Mrs. Dona[illegible]
5122 Pem[illegible]

D1499568

Dorothy Clark McKenna

THE CANDLE BOOK

Also by Carli Laklan

GIFTS FROM YOUR KITCHEN
(with Frederick-Thomas)

Carli Laklan

THE CANDLE BOOK

How to MAKE

DECORATE

DECORATE WITH

AND SELL CANDLES

M. BARROWS AND COMPANY, INC.

NEW YORK

To Elizabeth—whose life burns bright as a candle flame, warming all those who come to know and love her.

Published simultaneously in the Dominion of Canada by George J. McLeod Limited, Toronto.

Printed in the United States of America.

Library of Congress Catalog Card No. 56-9512

The Charm of Candlelight

EVERY WOMAN KNOWS the charm of candlelight. Plays have been written on the subject. Plots for stories have been built around it. Restaurants of note—as well as hostesses of reputation—wisely cater to it.

And more and more women are discovering the fun of making and decorating candles for their own homes, for gifts, and even as a means of making extra money. Here is a truly satisfying creative outlet which requires neither costly equipment nor expensive supplies. A few minutes' time and a few cents' worth of material can produce a homemade candle molded and tinted to suit both taste and occasion. Decorating possibilities—either for homemade or commercial candles—are practically limitless, and they range from amusing conversation pieces to elaborate works of art. Simple candle decorating can entertain the children on a rainy day. Candle creations help swell sales at church bazaars.

This book gives basic information necessary to making candles in your kitchen. You will find the instructions are simple and easy to follow. Dozens of ideas for decorating candles are offered: candles for special occasions, for special days, for specialized color schemes, and for moods of many manners.

You will find here, too, a generous number of candle arrangements for all occasions. Many of these have been created by artists and experts, and are offered for your approval.

For those who might like to turn their creative talents for making and decorating candles into a money-making hobby there is a chapter filled with ideas and suggestions which I think you will find helpful. They range from the prosaic matter of bookkeeping to the more lively matter of luring new customers. It's pin-money promotion!

And here and there throughout the book you will find some of the lovely and entertaining candle lore which highlights and underlines any discussion of candles.

I hope you have a pleasant time with this book, and a profitable one. My thanks to all of those who have contributed to it. And if I could make a wish for each of you, I think it couldn't be a better one than that the happiest moments of your life be warmed by candlelight—and so made glad. Maybe this book will help to make it so.

CARLI LAKLAN

April, 1956
Sea Cliff, Long Island
New York

Contents

Illustrations

Between pages 64-65

candle. Christmas decorations embellish a homemade cone candle. To the right, a well-burning candle made in a cottage cheese container. In the foreground, wax medallions for floating candles or to decorate pillar candles. A short taper decorated with miniature fruit. A pillar candle enlivened with Christmas bells.

Between pages 136-137
(in color)

Plate I. Jeweled patio candle by Avis Stendal; flower-studded sealing wax candle, and tall sealing-wax-decorated taper by Alice Jaffe; sequin-trimmed taper, shell-decorated pillar candle, and star-decked cone by Frederick-Thomas; homemade lavender candle and ice-blue driftwood candle by Michael Powers; at the right, another of Mrs. Jaffe's tapers.

Plate II. Foil moths flutter around a tall creamy taper; tissue balls, frosted Christmas-tree decorations and a lacy spray of gray caspia to complete the picture. Setting by Margaret Carrick, California.

Plate III. A red candle set in a Styrofoam ball tops the Italian glass bottle; a snowball candle stands at the base. Mexican straw beads spiral from one to the other. Setting by Margaret Carrick, California.

Between pages 144-145

13. A charming and easy-to-achieve arrangement of heather and pink carnations graced by flower tapers which run from pale pink to deep mauve. Candles by Colonial Candle Company. Photograph courtesy of Franklin Advertising Service.
14. An always-green setting for a pillar candle—the intriguing Candle Planter Bowl in copper and brass. From The Candle Light, Fair Haven, New Jersey.
15. Black that drips gold; white that drips silver, scarlet, or seven different colors—these candles spill their colored wax in particularly pleasing fashion. Candles by Ho-Car.

16. A kitchen garden conversation piece—the candles to harmonize with the chopping-block-and-vegetable décor. A red rose for the final fillip. Setting by Margaret Carrick, California.
17. Tall creamy beeswax candles which hold light within themselves; a yellow-toned spring bouquet in a green-blue glass container. Setting by Margaret Carrick, California.
18. For Easter entertaining: pink and yellow tapers in black metal holders, a basket full of flowers, an iron wire chicken basket holding colored eggs. Setting by Margaret Carrick, California.
19. For the entrance hall at Christmas time: welcoming candles in tin Mexican candlesticks; a charcoal pottery bell spilling bright-hued balls. Setting by Margaret Carrick, California.
20. A fat pink candle in a black wire candle ball, a from-your-garden arrangement of dahlias in a matching vase. Setting by Margaret Carrick, California.
21. Creamy white and delicate pink candles in a setting of frosty evergreens. The collector's-item Christmas decorations suspended nearby you can make yourself. Setting by Margaret Carrick, California.
22. Three white Taperlite candles dominate a supper setting. The dark green cloth provides a striking contrast for candles, pastel flowers and bone china. Candles and setting by Will & Baumer.
23. A snack buffet is highlighted by gay yellow Twistolites in turquoise pottery holders. Chrysanthemums, grapes and gourds form the centerpiece. The cloth is pale yellow. Candles and setting by Will & Baumer.
24. White Twistolite candles in green Bristol lusters on the table—green Taperlites on the chest in the background. The centerpiece is arranged in a "cardinal's hat"—this one once used by Ethan Allen. Candles and setting by Will & Baumer.
25. Dinner for two, softly lit by white Twistolite candles in massive Moorish candlesticks. Asters and purple grapes are arranged in an antique stove top. Setting and candles by Will & Baumer.

Between pages 160-161

26. An early American setting for a bayberry candle with its sweet scent and soft light. The foliage: cotoneaster. Candle and setting by Will & Baumer.
27. A formal arrangement for the mantel, featuring fall flowers and golden yellow Twistolite candles. Candles and setting by Will & Baumer.
28. A tin Colonial candlestick holds a sleek red Taperlite candle; evergreens, bright red gladioli and cotoneaster berries are backed by a pewter plate. Candle and setting by Will & Baumer.
29. A made-to-order match, with pineapple and citrus fruit decorating the candles. Both candles and setting by Lady Brett.
30. Summer-day suggestion: Delicately tinted candles with only the one floating in the cool crystal bowl lighted. Candles and setting by Lady Brett.
31. and 32. A selection of the unusual "special occasion" candles now available in shops—or for those who wish to have their own shops. These from The Candle Light, Fair Haven, New Jersey.
33. For autumn dining, Horn of Plenty candles and green grapes against a dark green cloth. Candles by Emkay. Setting by Norma Simpson.
34. The feature attraction is the Prism candle (center) which transforms itself into sculptured beauty as it burns. Setting by The Candle Light, Fair Haven, New Jersey. Prism candle by Victrylite Candle Company.
35. Decor-Lite's Magic Circle holders fit all candles. They may be used singly or in groups. Candle decorators find them useful for base-of-the-candle wreath decorations. Waxed flowers, miniature fruit and vegetable decorations, and so on, may be wired to them.
36. A corner of one of the country's best-known candle shops—begun originally in the corner of a grocery store, now housed in six rooms and with an international trade. The Candle Light, Fair Haven, New Jersey.

CANDLE-DIPPING

A candle's but a simple thing;
It starts with just a bit of string.
Yet dipped and dipped with patient hand,
It gathers wax upon the strand
Until, complete and snowy white,
It gives at last a lovely light.

Life seems so like that bit of string:
Each deed we do a simple thing;
Yet day by day if on life's strand
We work with patient heart and hand,
It gathers joy, makes dark days bright,
And gives at last a lovely light.*

CLARA BELL THURSTON

* From *Daily Word,* publication of Unity School of Christianity, Kansas City, Missouri.

I

In the Beginning

HOW TO MAKE ALL KINDS OF CANDLES

ACCORDING TO THE DICTIONARY, a candle is "a cylinder of tallow, wax, or other solid fat, containing a wick, to give light when burning." And by this definition, the earliest specimen is probably a fragment found at Vaison, not far from Avignon in France, and dating back to the first century A.D. On the face of it, a candle sounds something less than exciting, but it was a miracle which lengthened days, and lighted feasts; and let a mother walk softly through a room to check the safety of her sleeping infant.

Dictionaries have another definition for a candle: a light, a luminary. And there is charm in the words—and warmth, and romance, and loveliness. These never grow old. These light the candle's flame from ancient days to modern times.

Our great-grandmothers made their own candles out of strictest need. Today craftswomen and artists, hobbyists and home-businesswomen make candles for the enjoyment of it, and as a creative expression.

Recently I interviewed a sixty-eight-year-old widow, Mrs. Ellen Brown Combs, of Hempstead, Long Island. Her children are married. She has a small income—enough to live on without much jam on her bread. She is not an artist—nor has she ever been a "career woman." But she has the normal artistic ability most homemakers develop in the process of decorating their homes, giving parties, arranging flowers, and wrapping presents. And she was not, at sixty-eight, willing to retire to lavender and old lace.

She had tried a number of hobbies, and one day she turned to candlemaking. She wanted some special candles for friends who were celebrating their Golden Wedding anniversary, and she couldn't find them. So she made them. When I talked with her, her dining room had become her workroom. The round, old-fashioned table overflowed with decorative materials. Candles were lined on the sideboard, covered small tables and corner whatnots. From a box, she took a lovely pale-blue globe-of-a-candle decorated with delicate pastel flowers and tiny pearls. It was charming, and she was pleased that I liked it.

"I'll tell you a secret," she said. "The material for this candle cost me about 82 cents. It took me about 4 hours to make it—and what do I have but time? I am selling it for $4.00."

Her bright-blue eyes sparkled as she put the candle back in its box. "More fun than a rocking chair," she said. And I agreed.

Some weeks later I went to the fashionable East Fifties in Manhattan to visit the studio-showroom of two young decorators. One of their extra-income specialties is making and decorating candles. Neither is their main business—which is interior decorating. But candlemaking has become a profitable side line.

Then I have a young friend who can tell you almost anything you want to know about candlemaking. His name is Michael Powers, and he is fifteen years old. Some time ago an automobile accident temporarily restricted his active life. He turned to a number of shut-in hobbies—everything from raising hamsters, to teaching his pet parakeet to say, "Shep's a good dog, but he can't talk." One of these hobbies was candlemaking. Young Mike has made many of the candles described in this book.

Or I could tell you of a woman of fifty who has a profession of her own, but who—like most of us—believes that the handmade gift has special meaning, so she makes and decorates candles which her friends are happy to receive.

Making a candle is a good deal easier than making a good pie. And when decorating a candle it is really difficult to make a mistake. If, by chance, you don't like the candle you have molded, melt it down and start over. If you don't like the decoration you have used, it's usually simple to change it. Few crafts are so amenable—and few more gratifying. And so—*let's make some candles!*

BASIC FORMULAS—DO NOT SKIP

Many homemade candles are fashioned entirely from paraffin. It is inexpensive—easy to obtain. Candles made from it look beautiful, and burn merrily. Because of all this the instructions for candlemaking in *this* chapter are given in terms of paraffin. However, paraffin has a low melting point. Candles made entirely from it drip freely. You will have a considerable quantity of melted wax as they burn.

There are various materials which, added to paraffin, harden a candle and give it a higher melting point, such as stearic acid and beeswax.

Stearic acid or stearine, obtainable in crystal or lump form, is a fat from which the smoky—and odoriferous—glycerin has been extracted. It has a high melting point and is, therefore, valuable in candlemaking. Beeswax, which bees use for making honeycomb, has a melting point around 150° F. When it is sun-bleached, it is white. A small amount added to paraffin gives a fine finish to your candles, and improves them in general.

Following are the three Basic Formulas:

1. paraffin 66⅔ per cent
   stearic acid 33⅓ per cent
2. paraffin 60 per cent
   stearic acid 35 per cent
   beeswax 5 per cent
3. paraffin 55 per cent
   stearic acid 35 per cent
   beeswax 10 per cent

Be assured there is nothing rigid about these formulas. As a matter of fact, there are probably as many mixes as there are candlemakers. My formulas are simply to serve as guides. You might make a candle of 50 per cent paraffin and 50 per cent beeswax—or of all beeswax, or all paraffin.

You might use other waxes in your formula, too, ceresin, for instance, with a melting point from 130° to 170° F. This is also known as earth wax, cerin, cerosin, mineral wax, and purified ozokerite. It's sold in bags—graded according to melting point—and often used with paraffin in place of beeswax.

Carnauba wax is hard, brittle, yellowish-green, with a

very high melting point—up to about 196° F. Bleached and refined, it's almost white. This wax is expensive. Only a small percentage of it (say 2 or 3 per cent) is used in commercial candlemaking to harden ceresin and/or paraffin. Don't go in for this costly wax until you've perfected your techniques.

Candelilla wax—from a Mexican plant of that name—is harder than beeswax but not so hard as carnauba, and is expensive. If you wish to use it, about 5 per cent should be enough.

Other waxes which harden and give opacity include: Montan, Chinese or insect wax, synthetic waxes, such as B. naphthol, also Japan wax. This last is hard and brittle, but its melting point is low, from 122° to 133° F.

WAXES—WHERE TO GET THEM

Check with your local chemist and the chemistry department of your local high school or college. They may be able to get the special waxes in small quantities. Sometimes furniture refinishers and paint stores carry beeswax. If not, you may order in lots of 5, 10, 15, 20, etc., pounds from the following:

Bayberry Wax and Stearic Acid:
E. A. Bromund Company
258 Broadway
New York City, 7

Other special waxes mentioned, may be ordered from:
Frank B. Ross Co., Inc.
6 Ash Street
Jersey City 4, New Jersey

EQUIPMENT. All that's needed for candlemaking is: a double boiler, molds, a rotary egg beater (if you want frothy wax snow), a paring knife, an ice pick. Materials include a supply of wax (paraffin, or see the preceding formulas), colored wax crayons or oil paints, commercial wicking or soft white string, salt, and borax. All easy to procure and *not expensive.*

WICKS. Prepare these first—at least a day in advance of your candlemaking. Do 6 yard-long pieces of wicking at one time, these to be cut into desired lengths and used as wanted.

For 6 yards of wicking (or soft white string), dissolve 2 tablespoons of salt and 4 tablespoons of borax in 2 cups of water. Soak the string in this for about 2 hours. Then let it dry. The purpose of the salt and borax is to keep the string from burning down too rapidly or from "fizzing out" when the candle has been lighted.

To finish the wick, cut a piece about 2 inches longer than you will need for your candle, dip it in melted wax once or twice, and then hang it *up* to dry. Don't just drape it over a clothesline or you'll get a hairpin shape—and like pieced ribbon from a notions counter, this can be unhandy. The bend is sure to come just where you want it least. When the wax has stiffened, it's ready to use. The waxing, of course, can be done at the time you're making your candle. No need to melt extra wax for the process, and the unwaxed, treated string is easier to store, anyway.

Measure Memo: The larger the candle, the heavier the wick should be. If the wick is too small for the diameter of the candle, the flame melts the wax more quickly than it can burn, and the candle drips. Commercial wicking comes in sizes from 1 to 10. The first is a 15-thread wick, the last a 72-thread.

WAX PREPARATION. In making candles, always melt the wax in the top of a double boiler—or, barring that, set the pan with the wax in a skillet almost full of water. There is a reason for this: It's safer. Wax is inflammable and shouldn't be melted over direct heat. You don't want it ever to get smoking hot. If by chance wax should catch fire (and it won't if you take normal precautions), smother the flames fast by placing a tight lid on the pan. Don't pour water on it! A tight cover acts like a candle snuffer.

Did you know that it wasn't until the middle of the eighteenth century that candle snuffers were brought into use? One William Perkins, who lived in 1635, scorned such new-fangled notions; wrote indignantly to a friend: "If a man is to snuff a candle, he will first spit on his fingers." Forthright methods lost. Culture and candle snuffers came on apace.

COLORING. Ordinary wax crayons are excellent for coloring wax—easily available, inexpensive, and simple to use. With them, you can get colors from palest pastels to shining black. Allow about 2½ pounds of wax for a 1-quart mold. One crayon will give good color to this amount. Use two crayons for dark shades, and up to three crayons for a black candle; the same amount of white crayon for a white candle.

For delicate pastels, use two white crayons and from ¼ to ⅓ of a colored crayon. Or simply add a small amount of the colored crayon of your choice to the melted wax. The results will not be exactly the same, but still good.

In dime stores or art shops, you can often find jumbo wax crayons. These are a practical buy in white, black, clear red, yellow, blue, and green, the colors you will use most. By mixing these, you can get many different shades.

To tint candles, shave the crayons into the melted wax and stir well to blend the color. (See Illustration 3.) In developing special shades of your own, add your color a little at a time, stirring after each addition until you have exactly the tint you want. A color wheel, which you can buy in almost any art store, is a fine guide. It shows what to combine to get the shades you want.

For example: red plus yellow gives orange; red plus blue gives purple; blue plus yellow gives green. Half the amount of yellow to the red used will give Chinese red; half as much yellow as the amount of green gives chartreuse.

Oil paints may also be used to color candles. Buy large tubes of basic colors, and small tubes in every shade of the rainbow. Oils are, however, more expensive than crayons. And harder to use. You must stir them very well —and for quite some time—into the melted wax. An inch of oil paint (squeezed from the tube) will tint a quart mold. Three tablespoonsful will give a good clear color. For a deeper shade, double this amount.

MOLDING. When the wax has melted, the color been added, you are ready to fill the mold—and this can be anything from a milk carton to a liqueur glass. If you use a carton (or any other waxed-paper container), you do not need to grease or oil it, but be sure it is perfectly clean and completely dry.

Cover your worktable with newspapers and spread a few on the floor. (After your apprenticeship you'll no doubt dispense with the latter, but if you're a beginner, it's no bad idea. Wax is not the easiest thing in the world to clean up if it happens to splash.) Stand the mold in a baking pan, unless the mold is metal. Glass molds do break on occasion, and even a paper carton has been known to spring a leak at the most unlikely moment. The proverbial ounce of prevention has its merits. Do *not* work in your sink, for if you spill any wax, it may clog the drain.

Metal, plastic, or glass molds should—with a few exceptions which will be mentioned later—be greased carefully first. You can use vegetable shortening or oil, which I prefer—peanut, olive, or salad oil. It applies easily with a brush, covers well and thoroughly. It gives a shiny finish. Oil is particularly good for molds of intricate design, or when you are making medallions for decorations.

Pour the wax steadily and not too quickly into the mold —you don't want it to spatter. If you are using a large mold—and one which is *not* of waxed paper—you can let it stand in hot water 15 to 20 minutes after pouring. This keeps the wax from forming a film too quickly over the top, and lets air bubbles come to the surface. If the mold is of metal, you might put it in a slightly warm oven for the same amount of time—and the same reason. This isn't necessary with small molds, nor is it actually essential with any candle you may make.

Candles made in milk and cream cartons—or similar containers—will not have as shiny a surface as those made in glass or metal molds. But you can glue cellophane smoothly to the inside of the carton, and this will give a shiny surface. Or after the candle has been removed from the mold, you can dip it quickly into a deep pan of melted wax. This gives a smooth, gleaming surface. Stand the dipped candle on a paper to dry. You can also buff a candle with a waxed cloth to make it shine. But the business of giving a shiny surface to a candle isn't necessarily a part of making it handsome. I rather like the soft, unpolished surface which candles from milk and cream cartons have. They're particularly nice in pastel shades, and lend themselves well to decoration.

WAX SNOW. Making wax snow is a simple procedure. (See Illustration 4.) The snow can be used either for decorating or for molding candles. Melt the wax as for candlemaking. Tint it if you like. Let it cool until a ¼-inch film forms over the top. Then beat with a rotary beater. Or if you want a finer snow, beat with a fork. (See Illustration 5.) *Do* cover your work space with paper, for beaten wax is bound to spatter.

To mold a candle from wax snow, grease the mold and then pack the beaten wax in while it is still warm. (See Illustration 6.) Take care to fill the corners of the mold and pack the snow in well. When using snow—or froth, as it is sometimes called—for decorating, be sure the candle itself is completely set. To make the snow stick, apply it while it is warm, but not too hot. Set the candle you are decorating on a baking sheet or plate, and work rather quickly so that the snow won't harden too much before you have finished. (See Illustration 7.) Take pains to cover the candle evenly with the snow; otherwise the candle will look lopsided.

Apply snow of the same color as the candle, or in a contrasting or harmonizing color. A red candle, covered with white snow, for instance, will give an interesting effect as it burns. A deep-blue candle with a coating of ice-blue snow is a pretty sight. Large, square candles or good-sized, squat, round ones (like those made in cottage-cheese cartons), and globe candles are attractive in two colors—candle one shade, snow another.

Let candles harden well before you try to unmold them. Don't be impatient about this. Twelve hours is the minimum. If the weather is warm, harden the candle in the refrigerator. When the candle is ready, remove it carefully; if from a waxed carton, paper cup, mailing tube or the like, it may be easier to tear the carton away. With metal, plastic, or glass molds, run the tip of a paring knife around the edge, then tap the bottom of the mold gently to release the candle. Be careful about this. Hitting the mold too hard will whiten colored wax. But if you are using a medallion mold with a central design (for instance, a mold for an individual gelatin salad), don't be afraid to tap the center portion smartly. This will whiten it, and give an interesting decorative effect.

WICKS. To insert the wick, cut a length from your prepared string or wicking, leaving it a little longer than you seem to need. Heat an ice pick, and press it gently but firmly through the candle, reheating the pick in boiling water as often as necessary. After you have made the wick-hole through the candle, thread the prepared wick through it, the simplest method of inserting a candlewick.

> *Aging Action: Let candles cure 4 or 5 days before using them. This hardens the wax and gives it a chance to set perfectly. A bit like wine and cheese—and the combination, including the candle, is something to think about!*

MOLDS. There is one important thing to keep in mind when selecting molds: Can you get the molded candle out?

Very much the same story as that of the man who built a boat in his basement, forgetting the width of the door. Obviously, a mold which is smaller at the top than the bottom will not work. By the same token, a mold which has a wider span at its center or base won't either. And you'd be surprised how many times people forget this simple basic rule. But aside from it, anything goes.

There are a multitude of molds for candlemakers. Let's start with quart milk cartons—everyone has them. And they do make handsome candles. There is just one thing: the cartons tend to develop middle-aged spread when you pour in the wax. It's a good idea, therefore, to girdle them with two bands of adhesive or plastic tape—one band a third of the way from the carton's top, the other a third from the bottom. For a pint carton, one band is enough.

Mailing tubes can be used to make tall tapers. Because it is difficult to thread a wick through a thin candle, place the wick *before* you pour the wax. To do this, cut a small circle of cardboard and punch a hole in the center. Knot one end of the wicking, run it through the cardboard circle, and then tape the cardboard to the bottom of the mailing tube, knot outside. Pull the wick through the tube and hold it in the center of the tube as you pour in the wax, and for as long as it takes the wax to harden slightly at the top. If you stand the tube on ice as you pour in the hot wax, the wax will harden at the base almost at once, and help prevent run-out.

After the candle hardens, peel off the tube. Then polish the candle by rubbing it gently with a soft, waxed cloth. Or you can dip it into a deep container of hot wax—just in and out—holding the candle by the wick until the dipped surface has hardened. Here's one case where an extra-long wick is a help. You can clip the drying candle to a clothesline while it dries and so run no risk of marring the surface. Which would be a pity, because these fine, tall tapers have a graceful look, and burn brightly for a long, long time.

> ☙ *Minute Memo: Did you know that in early England special bed candles were made to burn just half an hour and then go out? Mothers were advised to send their daughters to bed with only one candle—and that a bed candle—to keep them from staying awake late reading such thrillers as, "Dolly Dell, the Duke's Doomed Daughter," and "Beautiful Blanche, the Betrayed Bride." Whether or not this stalwart advice worked, I do not know. But I suspect it was wasted. Times have not changed so very much.*

And now—from the general, which is necessary—to the particular, which is more exciting. So—to specific candles!

MILK-CARTON MARVELS. Remove the top of the container with a sharp knife. Wash and dry the carton carefully, and, if you wish the candle to be shiny, line it with cellophane. You will need 2 pounds of wax. (See Basic Formulas earlier in this chapter.) For a rose-pink candle—which is lovely—use one white crayon and one pink. Let the wax cool slightly before pouring it into the carton, and band the carton with adhesive to prevent bulging. (Refer to Molds.) Since wax shrinks a little as it cools, reserve some to fill the "well" which will appear as the candle hardens. Let the candle set over night in a cool place—and that means the refrigerator if the weather is its usual July or August self. The candle must be really hard before you remove it by tearing off the carton. Now you have one of the simplest candles for basic decoration.

Here are some other color ideas for 1 quart of wax:

Color	*Crayons*
Ice-Blue	1 white, 1 turquoise-blue
Black	3 black
White	3 white
Cream	3 white, ½ gold
Moss-Green	1 green, ½ red
Heliotrope	2 white, 1 lavender, ⅛ blue
Chinese-Red	2 clear red (no blue), 1 yellow
Burnt-Orange	2 gold, ½ brown
Deep-Jade	2 green, 2 blue

Sometimes it's fun to make candles in three shades of the same color—say, from deep- to pale-pink. Crayon proportions for a quart container would go like this: *Deep-Pink:* 2 pink and 1 white; *Medium-Pink:* 1 pink and 1 white; *Pale-Pink:* 3 white and ½ pink.

Three such candles make a pleasant decorative note for buffets, mantels, or dining table. Candles made in quart cartons are, of course, rather large and heavy. They don't look well on delicate tables, narrow ledges, or wherever they appear top heavy, but they are a type which can be handsomely decorated, as shown in Chapter 2.

Pint cartons require 1 pound of wax. (See Basic Formulas.) Half-pint cartons, which make attractive, rather stubby candles, require ½ pound of wax. To gauge amounts of color: For a pale-pink, half-pint candle, allow 1 white and ¼ clear-red crayon.

DRIFTWOOD CANDLES. These are decorator items and amusing to make—as you will discover. To make a pair, use just one clean, well-dried, quart milk carton, and 2 pounds of wax. (See Basic Formulas.) One turquoise crayon will give a lovely, delicate shade; 2 clear-yellow crayons add a sunlit note; ½ black crayon makes a silvery-gray.

Pour the melted wax into the mold. Let stand until the wax is set but still warm. Peel off the carton. Now pull the wax in two—much as you would in pulling taffy, twisting gently as you pull. Don't be too energetic—you want a tapering swirl, not a corkscrew.

You can mold the candle to suit your fancy as you work with it. The base of one candle will be the wax which was in the bottom of the carton; the base of the other, the wax which was in the top. This top and bottom wax has hardened slightly more than the rest, so handle these sections gently and don't twist here. These bases must remain flat and reasonably square. Remember, too, that the general trend of the twisted driftwood effect must be up, so that the candles will burn properly.

When you have molded your driftwood candles, let them harden overnight. To insert the wicks, use a length of copper wire, heated in very hot water as you normally would the ice pick used for inserting wicks. The copper wire is flexible, and with a little maneuvering you can pierce the center of the candles. If you have made a very twisted candle, you may find that you can insert the wick only part way through. This does not matter. Burn the candle that far, and if you like, do a second piercing and add another wick.

EMBOSSED CANDLES. These are attractive and unusual small candles. The designs may be as varied as the individual gelatin-salad molds—or whatever—you can find. You need two molds of any given pattern, for these candles are made in sections and sealed together.

You might, for instance, select a rectangular salad mold with a bunch of grapes stamped on the bottom. (The average individual mold holds about ¼ pound of wax—or ½ cup of melted wax.) (See Basic Formulas.) Use ½ dark-green crayon for a deep-jade color. Melt and color the wax, pour into small oiled molds. Let harden completely. If a well develops in the center, fill with molten

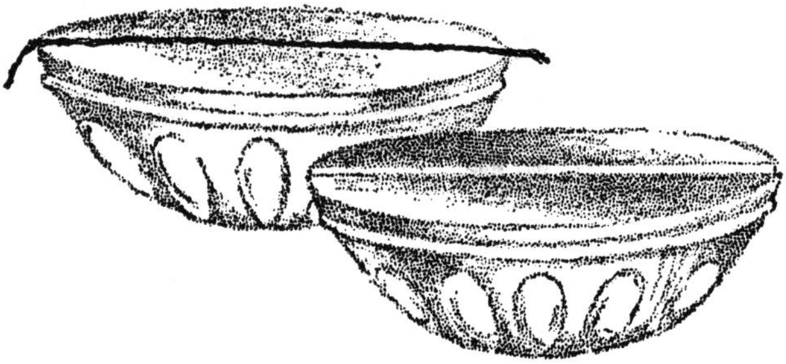

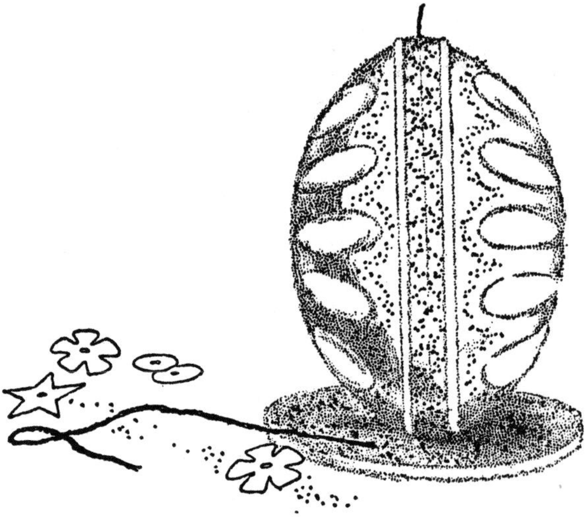

wax of the same color, and let reharden. Tap the molds gently to remove the candle-halves. If they seem reluctant, dip molds briefly in hot water, and then turn out wax.

Now with a paring knife, knitting needle, or even a nail file, cut a slight groove lengthwise along the flat surface of one of the wax forms. Lay the wicking in this. Let it protrude half an inch or so at the top—and be sure the grapes (or other designs) aren't upside down.

There are two ways to seal candle sections together: Coat the two flat surfaces quickly with hot wax of the same color as the candle, taking care not to spill any wax over the edges. Press the two halves firmly together, being sure that edges are even. Let the candle harden. Then trim off any wax which may have oozed out to mar the sides.

The second method is a little slower and a bit more trouble, but it gives a good solid sealing. Pour a thin sheet of colored wax, somewhat larger than the size of the molds you are going to seal together, onto a cold cooky sheet. Let the sheet set enough to handle but do not let it harden. Run a spatula under the sheet of wax. Place this on the candle half which holds the wick. Press down gently. Put the other candle half on top and press this down. Let set. Then trim off any excess wax with a sharp knife.

Most embossed candles must be mounted because the sides of the molds used are not straight and an unmounted candle will not stand properly. You can make a base of wax, in the same or a contrasting color. Use a plain, round, square or rectangular mold about ½ inch deep, and large enough so that the candle will fit into it properly. Let the base wax cool but not completely harden, then press the embossed candle firmly into it, taking care to set it straight. Now let the base harden completely before removing it from the mold. You can also make bases of modeling clay or Styrofoam.

Embossed candles may have a variety of designs depending on what the kitchenware departments offer, as playing-card motifs, birds, flowers, animals and geometric designs. Let the design suit your need or fancy, and color the candles as you wish.

SILHOUETTE CANDLES. It's the simplest thing in the world to make special-day candles in silhouette shapes, and they add a bright note to the decorating scheme. Hearts for Valentine's Day; clover candles for St. Patrick's; ears-of-corn for Thanksgiving; stars for Christmas; bells for New Year's, even fish candles for Lent. All you need do is find molds of proper shapes, and proceed as already indicated.

Heart, star, and clover candles need not be made in halves (like embossed candles), although they can be. You will probably like bell candles best if made in halves and sealed together. Ears-of-corn and fish types must be made so.

For the heart candle, insert the wick from the cleft of the heart to the point. Mount the heart on a wax base, as you do embossed candles. Run the wick for the star candle from any one point to the angle between the two points directly opposite. The candle is then mounted on these two points. Run the wick in the clover candle from the center top of one leaflet down through the stem, and mount the candle on the stem.

Make ear-of-corn candles in dishes intended for serving ears of corn, or in pans for baking cornbread—in either case, the mold is formed like half an ear of corn. Yellow crayon for coloring, of course, and when the two halves of the candle harden, insert the wick and seal the halves together as for embossed candles. Let harden overnight. The tip of the ear of corn becomes the candle top. With a sharp knife, pare down the "stalk-end" of the candle to fit your candleholder. And there you have it—as gay a candle as ever adorned a fall party table.

Make the fish candle the same way. Don't, incidentally, select large fish molds but look for individual ones. These candles must be mounted on a base like Embossed Candles.

> ☙ *Did you know that Indians of an earlier day dried smelts and then burned them as candles? Not to be recommended—except as a historical note.*

SNOWBALL CANDLES. These attractive candles usually make their appearance in shops during the holiday season but should not, I think, be limited to winter use. Make small ones, medium-sized ones, big jumbo ones—and make them not just in snowy-white and icy-blue, but in pale pink, lavender, gay yellow and soft-green. A whole array of unexpected colors will look as lovely on midsummer tables as the more usual white ones do on Christmas mantels.

To make a jumbo snowball, find a quart bowl so shaped that it will give you an almost perfect half globe, flattened only a little at the base. You will need 4¾ pounds of wax. (See Basic Formulas.) This amount of wax makes both halves of the candle, and the wax snow for coating it. For a pale-pink candle use ¼ pink crayon, ½ white one. (A pure-white candle requires 4 white crayons.)

Melt and color the wax. Make half of the candle and let it harden overnight. Leave the rest of the wax in the pan and remelt it for the second half. (This way you get no variation of color.) Of course, if you have two bowls the same shape and size, you can do both halves at the same time.

Remove the candle from the mold and make a groove from top to bottom on the flat side of one half. Place the prepared wicking. It should be a heavy type. Seal the halves together with additional melted wax. (See Embossed Candles for methods.)

Let the candle set another day, and then reheat the remaining wax. Let it cool until a film forms. Then beat with a rotary beater as directed for wax snow. When the wax is frothy, let it stand until it is just warm enough to handle, but not so hot that it will melt the smooth surface of the candle to which it is applied. You're apt to get a snow slide if the frothy wax is too hot.

Using a fork, and/or your fingers, cover the candle evenly with the snow, thickening it slightly around the base to give a firm foundation. Let harden and then clip the wick to the desired length. (See Illustration 7.)

For a medium-sized candle, use a pint bowl and 2⅓ pounds of wax. One turquoise crayon will color it. For a small snowball candle, custard cups give a good size. Allow 1⅓ pounds of wax, and 1 yellow crayon.

It looks pretty, too, to make the candle globe a deeper shade than the coating of wax snow. Or sometimes use two colors, as a deep-blue candle with white snow, a pale-green candle with yellow snow, or a lavender candle with pink snow. Sometimes add a package of glitter to the snow as you beat it. Any or all of these candles are attractive.

RAINBOW CANDLES. These take more time, but they are unusual. For molds, a Pilsener glass is good, and gives a tall, thin, cone candle. A tin funnel will make another cone. (Before starting, paste a square of waterproof adhesive over the hole in the bottom of the funnel to keep the wax from escaping.) A tall, metalware tumbler with straight sides will mold an attractive rainbow candle. Liqueur glasses make amusing little individual ones. To estimate amounts of wax: For a 1-cup container allow just over ½ pound of wax. (See Basic Formulas.)

Oil the molds. Select a variety of crayons to give you soft rainbow colors or bold Roman stripes. Color the wax a little at a time.

Pour a little of whatever color you want at the top of the candle into the mold. Let it harden for several hours or overnight. Then add the second color, *cooling the wax somewhat before pouring.* Let harden again. Continue adding colors in the order you have selected. Don't make all the stripes the same width and repeat colors if you like. Don't try to rush the hardening process. Do remember to cool the wax before pouring. If it comes straight from the stove, it may melt the previously poured color and give a fuzzy edge to your rainbow. Insert the wick in the usual way.

Timely Topic: King Alfred the Great, who reigned from 871 to 901, ordered the making of timekeeping candles. They were of beeswax, and the weight of 6 had to equal the weight of 72 pence. Each candle had 12 divisions marked on it, and when the 6 were lighted one after another, they burned 24 hours. Every time the flame passed a division mark on a candle, another 20 minutes had gone by.

SKYLINE CANDLES. Available molds are not apt to give you much variety in candle height, but this doesn't mean that tall candles can't be made at home. Two soup cans, for instance, will give you a round candle about 9 inches tall. Two straight-sided glasses will do about the same. Two pint cartons will give you a tall square candle, and so it goes. Candles are molded as already described, and then sealed together as for Embossed Candles. A half-pint container requires approximately ½ pound of wax. (See Basic Formulas.)

You will have joining marks where the candle sections are put together, but you can conceal these with a finishing wax dip if you have a deep enough container. You can run a line of wax snow or a narrow strip of wax over each joint. (Pour a ⅛-inch layer of wax into a square cake pan. Cut in strips, wind around the candle when the wax is set but not completely hard.) Or use decorations to cover the joints.

Here's another intriguing skyline candle: Select a mold about 3 inches deep, and if square-topped, about 2 inches per side. Choose one smaller at the bottom than the top and of a graceful shape. (Small plastic vases make good molds.) When you select a mold, try to visualize how a series will look stacked one on top of another, pagoda-fashion. Make from 3 to 5 candles in the same mold, depending on the final height you want. When the sections are hard, seal them together with extra wax, one on top of the other, wide side down each time. Be careful when lining them up, or you'll have a Leaning-Tower-of-Pisa effect. Go easy when you put in the wick—a long knitting needle is a good tool.

Block skyline candles are fun, too. Use a square mold, about 2 inches wide on each side. A cream container will do, but make a guide line on the outside so that you will put in only about 1½ inches of wax for each block. Eight blocks will give you a 12-inch candle. Make the blocks of different colors, if you like. When all are completely hard (and don't forget to fill the wells which appear in the tops), stick the blocks together with extra wax, one on top of another, but angled a little so the corners are never flush. Be careful to keep each block exactly centered over the previous one. (If you make the wick-hole in each block first, you can line up the blocks by using a knitting needle.) Insert the wick as usual.

> *Did you know that the Early American settlers announced events, such as a prayer meeting, by saying it would be "at early candlelight?"*

CANDELIGHTS. They *are* rather delightful, too, and something different for you to try—little candles which look like lights and are made with a minimum of effort. You can vary the patterns, but the basic idea is the same.

For example: Use an aluminum-foil dish which an individual frozen meat pie comes in, and a highball glass. Each will hold approximately ½ pound of wax. (See Basic Formulas.) Oil both molds well. Use a dark-colored wax for the base—deep-green, say—and fill the foil dish with this. Use a lighter shade—chartreuse, for instance—for the top which is made in the highball glass. Be sure to let the wax cool before pouring it into this, or any other, glass mold. After they harden fill in the wells with extra wax. When all is completely hard, seal the parts together with extra wax—placing the section made in the foil dish right-side-up and inverting the one from the highball glass, centering it on the foil-dish section. When set, insert the wick.

Now you need three jumbo-sized paper clips to form legs. At three equidistant points on the foil-dish section make slots in which to insert the clips. Turn the candle upside down. Fill the slots with warm wax. Let stand until nearly set, then force the end of a paper clip into each, letting about half an inch protrude. Be sure this is the double-loop end of the clip. Take care to get the three paper-clip legs exactly the same depth into the wax, and at the same angle, so that your candle will stand straight. Seal each in place with a little extra wax, and let harden. Then your little candle will stand on its paper-clip legs in fine fashion.

You may make similar candelights with other molds—a saucedish and soup can, for instance. A deep saucer and a glass. (In this case, invert the saucer part of the candlestick and seal the glass-molded part to it.) A salmon can and a frozen-fruit-juice can give another shape. You can use other things for legs, too—golf tees, for instance. Or glass drawer-pulls. Candelights make special little conversation pieces, and are fun to do.

FLOATING CANDLES. Molding floating flower candles can be an art in itself. Your own experiments will lead you to all manner of charming flowers. The directions here are simply for a basic guide.

You will want a small round bowl or mold (about 2 to 2½ inches in diameter), an 8-inch-square cake pan, a small heart-shaped cooky cutter—all well oiled.

Melt and color the wax—lavender, say. Pour a thin layer (not quite ¼ inch thick) into the cake pan. Keep the rest of the wax warm and add a little more colored crayon so that it will be a slightly deeper shade.

When the wax in the cake pan is set but still pliable,

cut out the heart shapes with the cutter. You may find that you need a sharp paring knife to help cut through the wax. Lift the hearts out carefully, one by one, and press them, cleft-side up around the inside rim of the bowl. Let the rounded tops extend a bit above the rim. Overlap them a little, and mold them slightly with your fingers to give a petal effect.

Let the slightly darker wax cool to the film stage. Then almost fill the center of the bowl with it. Have ready a bit of yellow wax, and pour a few drops of this into the center of the flower before the wax has hardened.

Let harden and insert the wick. A few dots of black crayon may be put in a circle around the wick to complete the flower. (Just melt the tip of the crayon a little and draw in the dot.) This, then, is one example of cutting, shaping, and molding petals. It is really modeling in wax.

FLOATING PINWHEELS. These are fun to make and intriguing to use. You'll need small, star-shaped molds, birthday candles, and some wax snow in a color to harmonize with the candles. Oil the molds, whip the wax with a fork, and press it into the molds, taking care to fill all corners. Before the wax snow sets, stand a birthday candle (not in a holder) at each corner of the star. Let harden. When the pinwheels are floated, the birthday candles are, of course, lighted.

Auctioneer: In Samuel Pepys' England, bidding at auction was timed by a candle. A half inch or so of candle was lit to start the bidding, and the winning bid was the last one made before the candle flickered out. The custom is still followed in some places in England today, and you may still hear bidders being warned to "Hurry, now! The candle's guttering!" Incidentally, the rental of "church acres" has been disposed of in this way for centuries.

ADDED ATTRACTIONS. There are many other molds which make charming candles. Here are a few for you to consider:

Graduated metal measuring cup—the kind which goes from small diameter to large in a series of widening steps. Requires approximately ½ pound of wax.

Bar butter dish—use only the cover, and select one with a design pressed into the top of the glass. Make two and seal together. Stand on a square base of wax or modeling clay. Requires about 1 pound of wax.

Round plastic refrigerator dish—quart size, and shaped like a cottage-cheese container (which you can also use, of course. The plastic gives a smooth finish). Approximately 2 pounds of wax here, and if you decide to make a black candle, which is nice in this size and shape, use 2½ black crayons.

Fluted gelatin molds—about the size of custard cups. It takes about ¾ pound of wax to fill one. Two can be put together to make an attractive round candle. If the fluting swirls, you'll get one effect. If it runs vertically, and you use orange coloring, you'll have a Halloween pumpkin. Paint on a face with melted black crayon if you like.

Small plastic flower vases—in many shapes and sizes to make interesting candles. One we found had a fluted edge about half an inch deep, a square top, convex sides, and a half-inch-deep square base. This mold required approximately 1 pound of wax.

FRUIT CANDLES. Dime stores have wall plaques (meant to bedeck kitchens) each of which has an ornamental plastic half fruit in it—an apple, orange or pear. These are embossed so when you pry the fruit away from the plaque and use it as a mold, you get all the markings. Make two halves, of course. (They require approximately ½ pound of wax in all.) A little ingenuity is needed to put the halves together. Place the wick and seal the halves as you would for Embossed Candles. When you seal the halves, the leaves won't match. So from one half, carefully pare away the impression of the leaf. Then dip the fruit quickly in a wax bath of the proper color, and let drain. With a little melted green wax, coat the partial leaf which your fruit candle now has. Then with more green wax, form an extra leaf and place it so that it overlaps the partial leaf already molded. This sounds complicated, but really is not, and the finished product is gay and attractive.

> *You can make plaster-of-Paris models to use as molds for candles—of candlesticks, cologne bottles, and the like. Mix the plaster of Paris according to directions on the package, taking care that it is smooth. Grease whatever you wish to use as a mold. Make the molds in two halves. When set and removed, coat the inside well with shellac (several coats of spray shellac or plastic spray). Mold your candles as you would Embossed Candles, and finish in the same way.*

EASTER EGG CANDLES. These are fun favors, and not at all difficult to do. Your mold is an egg shell. Tap the large end gently to crack the shell, and pick off just enough of it to make a hole about ¾ inch across. Work carefully so that you don't crack the rest of the egg. Shake the egg from the shell. (The day you make these will be a good day for a soufflé.) Rinse the shell with cold water.

Hold the shell broken side up against a breadboard and

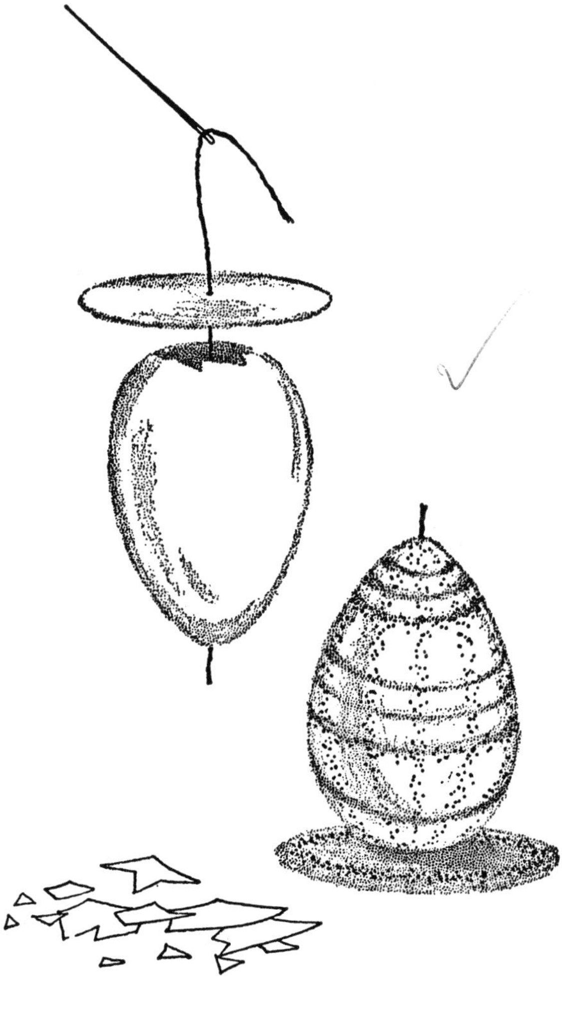

pierce the small end with a darning needle. Cut a circle of cardboard about 2 inches in diameter, and pierce the center of it. Now thread a prepared wick (a fine one) through the needle hole in the bottom of the shell, up through the shell, and then through the cardboard circle. Leave about ¼ inch of wick sticking out of the needle hole in the egg, and fasten it down with a piece of plastic tape which will also cover the needle hole.

Stand the egg in a little bed of modeling wax to hold it upright. Fill with melted wax, colored as you desire. (It takes from ¼ to ⅓ cup of wax for each egg candle.) Hold the wick straight as you pour. If the wax shrinks as it cools, add a little more. When the wax is set but not hard, push the cardboard circle into place directly over the broken end of the egg, and press it gently against the wax. (This will become the base of the candle; the cardboard will hold the candle up.) Let harden completely. Clip off extra wick above the cardboard. Untape the other end. Peel off the shell. And you may finish these egg candles with any kind of gay decoration you like. Cover the cardboard with decorations, too.

You can also make Easter eggs in an egg cup—egg-sized ones in the egg-holder section, larger ones in the other end. Make two halves, and seal as in Embossed Candles. Sometime try coloring the egg candles white, then dipping them in a color bath. With Easter-egg candles made this way, put the wicks in when the candle is finished. Modeling clay can be used as a base.

In the Medieval Church, tradition demanded that candles be made of beeswax—and the tradition dates to the charming legend of the virgin bees coming to earth directly from heaven. The

Church of Rome still requires that altar candles, the light of which is "nourished by the melting wax which the parent bee produced," shall be made of at least 65 per cent beeswax.

COLOR SWIRL CANDLES. The mold doesn't matter, and the method is simple. Melt wax and let it cool slightly. Have ready varicolored flakes shaved from crayons—in colors which harmonize. Pour the wax slowly and carefully into the mold, sifting in the colored flakes as you pour. Don't stir, and don't move the candle until the wax is set.

COLOR DRIP CANDLES. You can get a varicolored effect from a burning candle by melting holes through inch lengths of colored crayons with a hot knitting needle, and stringing them on a prepared wick. Dip in wax to hold the crayons in a straight line. Work a hole through the center of the candle with a hot ice pick. (It has to be large enough to take the string of crayons.) Insert the crayon string and pour in a little wax to set it. As the candle burns, the various colors melt and drip, so better have a white candle if you choose a gay variety of colors. At any rate, pick colors which go together.

DIPPED CANDLES. Time was when great-grandmother made the year's supply of candles by dipping them, and since it takes from 20 to 30 dips to get a fair-sized taper, this represented no little chore. But a lovely wealth of American history and tradition has been written by light from softly-glowing, hand-dipped candles. Our forefathers' homes were lighted by them. The first children born on American soil learned their lessons and said their prayers by candlelight. Women in log cabins on western plains mended and darned by precious candlelight. The Declaration of Independence was signed by candlelight. The first reception at the White House, in 1809, was lighted by a thousand flickering tapers.

And today when we give the small gift of hand-dipped candles to a friend, we give not just the gift but part of all the history—great and small—which has been lived by their bright flames.

> *Did you know that the Colonial Candle Company in Cape Cod, where the Pilgrim Fathers lit their first candles, is one of the few concerns still making candles by the process of hand-dipping?*

To dip your own candles, you need wicking or soft string, cut about 6 inches longer than the actual candle length desired. Commercial wicking may be rather thick and tight. Untwist it and separate two or three strands, retwisting them for your dipped candle. You need a short length of stick, too, or wooden wand about 12 inches long, and wax, of course. (See Basic Formulas.) And you need two tall, deep, wide-mouthed jars. Melt the wax, fill one jar, and stand it in boiling-hot water. Stand the other jar in ice cubes and fill it with cold water.

Tie one end of the wicking to the stick—the purpose being ease of handling. First dip the wick in the wax. Pull it out, and let the wax harden in the air. Dip it into the cold water. Let drain *completely.* Dip again, let harden, then dip into the water, and drain. Keep this up until you have the size taper you desire. Then hang it by the extra wick to a clothesline until it has hardened.

If you want a candle to taper gently, don't dip the candle all the way into the wax each time. The first several times, of course, go clear into the wax to form the core. After that sometimes dip the candle only halfway, sometimes two-thirds. You can tell as the candle grows how deep to sink it each time into the wax, and with a little practice, you will be able to make expertly tapered candles.

If the dipping wax begins to harden, reheat it, and reheat the water in which the container stands. And need I say that throughout all of this, it is wise to have the work space well covered with paper?

If you want your candle to be cone-shaped (and you might like such a hand-dipped green candle at Christmas to turn into a Christmas tree), tie a double knot in the end of the wick. This will make the wax grow faster there. Then graduate the dippings to get the desired shape.

You can dip varicolored drip candles by having ready two or three jars of different colored wax. Dip two or three times into one color before going on to the next. Alternate as you like. This is a good use for melted candle ends, saved through the year.

MEMORY CANDLES. There's a family tradition connected with these, and one you may adopt if the members of your family are separated. It goes back to the sharing of the hearth fire, which in olden days was the symbol of home—its very heart. Coals carried from the hearth of the parental home lighted the first fires in the new homes of married sons and daughters.

When children began to move too far away to carry live coals, the old tradition substituted candles, and the candle flame became the symbol of the dual hearth flames. Many families now exchange candles at Christmas time, and on

Christmas Eve, sons and daughters who live in distant cities light the candles, knowing that at home another candle burns for them. Any candle can carry on this tradition. One which you make, one which you buy, one which you decorate. But these memory candles have a special sentimental value of their own. Here's how they're made:

Select an attractive bottle, one which will make a candle of interesting shape. It's best not to take one with a long neck (or at least not to fill the neck), because chances of breaking the candle when removing it are too great. You can find jugs and jars which have good shapes. A pinch bottle is interesting. A cider jug, a wine bottle. Best that the glass be not *too* heavy.

Next, place the prepared wick. Tie a small weight to one end of the wicking, a rod which can be fixed in place across the top of the bottle on the other end. The wick, when in place, should hang without slack, and you accomplish this by rolling the wick around the rod until it is the right length. Don't try to cut your wick just the depth of the bottle. You need a few inches of leeway so you can roll the rod away when pouring in the wax.

The candle bottle is ready now, and the filling of it goes on during the year. When you celebrate a birthday, when the birthday wishes have been made and the candles blown out, melt down the candle ends, remove the wicks, and pour the melted wax into the bottle. If candles are used on the dinner table for some festivity, melt down what remains, too, and add this wax. When the candles which stand on the mantel have burned down, melt the stubs and add these to your candle. And so it goes—with the bottle slowly filling with the wax of candles which have been part of your own living. As you pour in the wax each time, roll the rod away, but replace it while the wax is still molten, so the wick will be straight when the wax sets.

Your candle will have many colors—a patchwork quilt of a candle. And perhaps when you send it on to some member of your family who is away from home, you'll want to add a note: "Jean's birthday candles were pink—the same as her dress. . . . The night the Matthews came to dinner, I had red roses from the garden on the table, and we had ivory-colored tapers. Peach pie, too—the first of the season. We thought of you. . . . The green comes from the candles we had burning on the mantel the night your dad lit the first fall fire in the little room. We just sat there awhile, watching the fire, and talking about the way you youngsters used to hunt 'pictures' in the glowing coals. . . ."

Every such candle holds a wealth of memories which have been part of family life. And this is good. Sometimes today, we think, families take little time to sit, remembering, and resharing. But both are part of what each child carries away with him when he goes out to live his own life. Part of laughter and tenderness . . . . the look in a child's eyes, finding a fairy ring caught in the grass . . . . the smell of gingerbread, baking in the kitchen . . . . your father's voice, waking you Christmas morning, calling "A Merry Christmas" . . . . your mother's smile.

Small things? Not at all. They are the greatest and the richest—all of the things which money cannot buy, and neither time nor distance will erase. These are the lasting things, and if a homemade candle and its bright, clear light, helps to perpetuate them, then it needs nothing more to recommend it. Nor asks for more.

By Christmas time the memory candle is ready to go

on its way, carrying its message. It must first be removed from the mold—and care is needed. Clip the rod from the wick. Break the bottle from the candle. There are those fortunate people whose households boast a glass cutter, and if so they can cut the glass away neatly and simply. (They can also use much fancier bottle shapes, because getting the candle out is no problem!) Barring this, strike the bottle smartly on the bottom with a hammer, shattering the glass. Pick away the glass fragments carefully. The fewer times you have to strike the bottle, the better, for the blows will mar the candle. (Don't worry, you can dip it quickly in a bath of colored wax to give it a finishing touch. It will still burn down showing all the colors you have put into it.)

If the glass is not too thick, you can sometimes break it by putting it in the refrigerator overnight and then plunging it suddenly into boiling water. (Make a tea-towel sack for this operation, please.) When the mold has been removed, and the candle dipped or polished with a waxed cloth to give it a soft, smooth finish, when the wick has been clipped, then it is ready to be sent on its mission. And may it burn through many hours of happy memories!

In Jewish homes the Sabbath begins at sundown Friday. The table is spread with a dinner cloth. Two loaves of challah, covered with a white embroidered cloth, have been placed at the head of the table. The Sabbath candlesticks, each with its fresh white taper, have been placed in the center of the table. There are always two candles —sometimes there is one for each member of the family. A goblet to be filled with wine for Kiddush stands near the challah.

As the sun goes down, the mother lights each candle while the children watch. She stands for a second with her hands spread toward the flames, then places her hands over her eyes. She recites a benediction silently, then as she looks at the candles, whispers a meditative prayer. Mother and children greet each other with "Gut Shabbas!", and the greeting is repeated as the men return from the synagogue. And the quiet ceremony of lighting the candles is warm and impressive.

CANDLE CARVING. If you are adept at carving—and practice is the best method here—you can carve candles to suit your fancy. It's like the soap carving we used to do in school. Large, *undipped* candles are more easily worked than slender tapers. Use a very sharp knife, a single-edged razor blade, or carving tools. Select a simple, clean-lined design. Spread papers on the floor, and every once in a while scoop up the wax chips so they don't scatter.

Select an allover design. First cut paper of a size to cover the candle. Then draw in the design—flowers or leaves and tendrils, for instance—freehand or trace a pattern from magazine or book. Keep the design simple. Think of it as outline, not in terms of shading and color.

Clip or pin the paper pattern in place around the candle. With a heated needle, prick in guide lines for the design by sticking the hot needle through the paper along your pencil lines. Don't make the dots deep—just enough so you can see them. Remove the paper pattern, and finish the decoration with your carving tools. Use a light sure touch. Make the lines of varying depths to give a pleasant sculptured look.

Instead of a floral design, you can carve names and dates —as for birthday or anniversary—geometric designs, figures of animals or people, scenes, or whatever you feel capable of handling. If you are a beginner, keep it simple.

The candle which burns with a well will preserve your design better than a very slim candle. And in such a candle, the carved design takes on interesting depth and shading as the candle burns down. But a tall carved taper can also be quite lovely. Buff with a waxed cloth to finish. Need I add that you do not need to make the candles you carve unless you want to. Commercial candles in all shapes and sizes are available.

BAYBERRY CANDLES.

Bayberry candles when burned to the socket,
Bring friends, and good fortune, and gold to the pocket.

Such, at least, is the tradition which has come down to us since that day, 300 or so years ago, when the Pilgrims of Massachusetts discovered the fields of bayberry bushes, and found that the berries were covered with a gray-green wax which had a pleasant, pungent odor.

You can, if you live where bayberries grow, make Christmas bayberry candles just as the early New Englanders did when they began the custom of using them during the holiday season. The berries are stripped from the bushes in September. And about 1½ quarts will make an 8-inch candle.

To release the wax, cover the berries with water, and boil for about 5 minutes. Work with small batches. The wax rises more easily then and handling is simpler. After the boiling period, set the berries in a cool place until the wax rises to the top of the kettle. Then skim off the wax.

Set it aside and go on boiling and skimming until you have used up all the berries. Then remelt the wax you have collected, let the impurities settle, strain, and store it in tightly sealed containers until you are ready to make your bayberry candles. Don't make them too far ahead of Christmas, for they lose fragrance.

You may either dip or mold bayberry candles, and if you do not have an old-fashioned candle mold—there *are* a few people who do!—you may fashion one from tin or even from Bristol board. Thread the wick through the mold, and fasten it, with half an inch to spare, at the small end of the mold with a little square of adhesive plastic tape. This will hold the wick in place and keep the wax from leaking out when you pour the candles. Have ready a piece of cardboard with a center slit of ¼ inch or so.

Melt the bayberry wax, and fill the mold, holding the wick straight. Then draw the free end of the wick through the slot in the cardboard, pull it tight, and adjust the cardboard over the mold so the wick holds straight and in the center of the candle. Clip a clothespin on the wick just above the cardboard to hold all secure.

Let the wax set, then stand the mold in the refrigerator to harden. If the wax shrinks, fill in with a little extra. To unmold, dip the mold into boiling water briefly, then pull the candle out and hang it, by the wick, to dry. If a Bristol-board mold has been used, simply peel it away.

Trim the wick. Then store the candles in a tight container until you want to use or give them. Proper storing helps to preserve the bayberry fragrance.

Note: Bayberry wax may be purchased commercially.

PERFUMED CANDLES. You can add a few drops of perfume to the somewhat-cooled wax before you pour it. Or add fragrant oil of sandalwood, patchouli (of the mint family), pine-tar, or vetiver (from a tropical grass or root). Oil of cloves will give a spicy scent. Eucalyptus oil a pungent clean odor. (All oils are obtainable at chemists.) Some candlemakers soak wicks in oil or perfume before coating them with wax, instead of adding scents to the cooled wax.

FLAMEBRIGHT CANDLES. Candles will burn with colored flames if wicks are treated with salts of copper, barium, strontium, or some such. A chemist—or the local high-school chemistry laboratory—will help you get them. If you want the wick to burn down with several colors, treat sections of it with the different salts.

CITRONELLA CANDLES. Make your own candles to keep away summer insects. Simply drill four holes about 1½ inches deep around the wick of a stubby candle (say, cheese-glass size). Make the holes with a hot ice pick, and fill with citronella. Seal over with a little melted wax. Small white candles which cost about five cents work admirably. So will commercial vigil lights.

Here, then, you've had cues and suggestions for the fine craft of candlemaking. You'll make many other candles, I know, and may they all be lovely.

And did you know that candles were once so very precious that they were snuffed out with a prayer for their renewal?

Neither do men light a candle,
and put it under a bushel,
but on a candlestick;
and it giveth light unto all
that are in the house.

MATTHEW 5:15

II

Designed by Decoration

HOW TO DECORATE THE CANDLES YOU BUY OR MAKE

A HANDSOMELY DECORATED CANDLE makes either a lovely gift or a charming decorative note for your own home. Most of us have admired those sold in shops, and some of them are surely works of art. They have a way, those specially decorated candles, of being pretty expensive, too, so it's a satisfying thing—in more ways than one—to be able to do your own decorating.

You can decorate either the candles you have made or those you have purchased. In the shops, you will find many shapes, styles, and colors. Browse through these candle shops and departments. Your problem will not be to find candles on which to work, but to limit your choice.

I have said this before—but will repeat it: You need not be an artist to decorate your own candles. If you are, of course it is on the plus side. But if you have never done any creative art work in your life, and would like to, candles may well be a good place to begin. You may start hesitantly, buying a little bright gold or silver glitter, coating a candle with melted wax, sifting the glitter over it—and being pleased with the result. You may begin by tacking on a few sequins in hit-or-miss fashion. Then one day you will find yourself searching the shops for all manner of decorative items. A picture in a magazine will give you an idea. A friend says: "Why don't you—?" You're an adventurer in a brand-new craft—and it *is* fun.

All of us need some form of creative expression. We find it in the garden we grow, the cake we bake, the home we decorate, the packages we wrap. The upsurge of Sunday painters has shown our strong desire for more than technocracy. The swing toward do-it-yourself projects is another example. We are not robots. We never will be. And in creation, we find satisfaction for our souls.

Children, of course, know this from earliest playtime. Give a child a box, a pan, an empty spool. From such things, he will create a marvelous array of imaginary things.

Any form of creation gives us this yeasty youth. Candle-making and decorating is only one of many. But it's simple to do, within our means, and a craft which moderate skill can manage beautifully—which talent can turn exquisite. So it can be for all of us.

In searching for items with which to decorate candles, haunt the novelty counters of dime and department stores. These days they offer a wealth of opportunity: packaged sequins and beads, glitter, ready-worked medallions, plastic crystals, jet and rhinestones, metallic braid and tape. Visit stationery stores for copper brads, wire staples, colored gummed labels, paper clips. Hardware shops yield fine copper chains, copper wire, ornamental upholstery nails, washers. Go to the departments where hat trimmings may be found—flowers, leaves, ornaments, butterflies, jeweled bees. Costume jewelry will be useful: necklaces, rings, pins, brooches, clips. If you lose a stone from an inexpensive piece of costume jewelry, if a string of beads breaks, if one earring is lost, save what remains. Other stones may be pried from the one-stone-lost piece and set into a candle. A single earring may be just what is needed to give a glamorous touch.

Buttons make good decorations too. Medallions cut from gold and silver paper doilies come in handy. Sheets of metallic paper lettering. Odds and ends of Christmas tree ornaments. Shells and colored pebbles from aquarium shops. The small charms children get from gum machines. In short, once you start making a list, you scarcely know where to stop. And part of the fun is, of course, this new field of discovery. You'll find yourself eyeing the most unlikely subjects—wondering just what you could do with it in a candle decoration. Part of creation at work!

So, let's begin our specific decorations. Yours to follow, to copy, to adapt—to use for your own inspiration.

GLITTER CANDLES. Buy the basic candle, or make it. Dip the candle quickly into a bath of melted wax of the same color. Let drain briefly on waxed paper or aluminum foil, but don't let the outer wax harden. Sprinkle on glitter in allover fashion. Presto, a gay and sparkling candle.

Variations: Sift silver glitter in an uneven icicle pattern over the top half of a candle which is about the size and shape of a cottage-cheese container. Sift gold glitter over the rest of the candle.

Or dip and drain a square, squat candle. Sprinkle, sparingly, a light sifting of gold or silver glitter. Then with varicolored glitter make swirls in free-form fashion over all. Work quickly. The wax hardens fast.

Candles covered with wax snow can be glitter-decorated. Simply sift it on before the snow has set.

STENCIL CANDLES. Make first a stencil pattern. Cut a paper—one with a hard finish and reasonably stiff—of a size to cover the surface of your candle. On it draw an allover pattern which can be cut out to form the stencil. It might, for instance, be polka dots of various sizes. It might be of geometric forms. It might be an old-fashioned snowflake pattern. To make snowflakes, you fold the paper in half; then fold it in half again. You can cut now for a simple snowflake, or fold the paper a third time from the center point for a more complex snowflake. If you aren't sure of your technique, just practice a few times and the knack will soon come to you. For a folded-and-cut stencil, use ordinary paper. Then trace onto the stiffer paper. Cut out with a razor blade.

When the pattern is cut out, pin it in place around your candle (and large square or round candles are the easiest to do in this fashion, but not the only kind which may be used).

Have a little pot of melted wax on hand. Paint the hot wax onto the candle through one cut-out part of the design. Sprinkle on glitter at once. Continue until the whole design has been done. Try not to run the wax over the paper pattern. But if you have run over, cut through the wax at the edges of your design with a razor blade before trying to remove the stencil. If the candle is marred because of such runovers, touch them up with a little melted wax and additional glitter. Let the decorations harden.

You can do endless variations with this kind of thing. For instance, you might write Happy Birthday around the candle. Or a name or date. You might wish to make a lodge or club emblem. Or finish the candle in a leaf design. Or whatever.

In making the stencil, don't forget the basic rule: Each part of the design must be joined to the main area of paper or the design will fall apart. In cutting the letter O for example, small "bridges" of paper must be left at top and bottom, otherwise the center of the O will fall out.

Glitter stenciling makes a sparkling embroidery against the plain background color of a candle. You may adapt this method of decoration, and paint in the stencil pattern with melted wax crayons if you like. For easy use, melt them in toy muffin pans. Work very carefully, and try not to run the crayon over the edges of the cutout pattern. In fact, if you can keep your painting just inside the paper outline, not touching it anywhere, you will be better off. Unless you have a sure eye for color, it's best to make first a scale color drawing of your design as a guide. This way, you will be sure that the colors you select are what you really want.

As a postscript: Stenciled borders can be run around top and bottom of heavy candles either in glitter or colored crayon.

GLAMOUR CANDLES. These are the sequin-trimmed candles—wonderfully easy to make, and charming indeed. Sequins come in all shapes, sizes, and colors. Do get a variety of them. They're fastened to candles by short pins.

Common pins can be clipped short with a wire cutter. You may run pins first through a tiny bead, then through the sequin and into the candle.

Most frequently seen are the glamour candles which have a variety of sequins pinned in pleasing, random fashion over the candle sides. There's no rule to this. You may use many or few, all one color or a variety of colors; all one shape or of many shapes and varying sizes. If you like, you can have a trial run by placing the candle on its side, then laying the sequins in place without pinning them, shifting them about until you get the desired effect. If, in pinning, you make a mistake, simply pull the pin out. With a hot knife quickly smooth over the pinhole, this will do an effective mending job.

For a change: Try a geometric pattern. You might begin with a diamond pattern. Draw the lines on tracing paper cut to fit the entire surface of the candle. Pin the pattern in place around the candle. Make a pinprick at each crossing of the lines (thus at each corner of every diamond). Remove the paper, and pin on the sequins as the marks indicate. You may decide to use two types of sequins, alternating them on the diamonds. Or you might like to shade the colors, beginning with dark sequins around the base of the candle, grading to pale ones at the top.

Or select a heavy, square candle: Mark the top center point on each side. Then pinprick an inverted V on each side. To do this, lay the candle on one side, place a ruler from the center point to one lower corner, and make dots at intervals along the ruler's edge with a pin. Repeat to the other corner. And then repeat the whole operation on each of the other sides. Pin sequins along these lines.

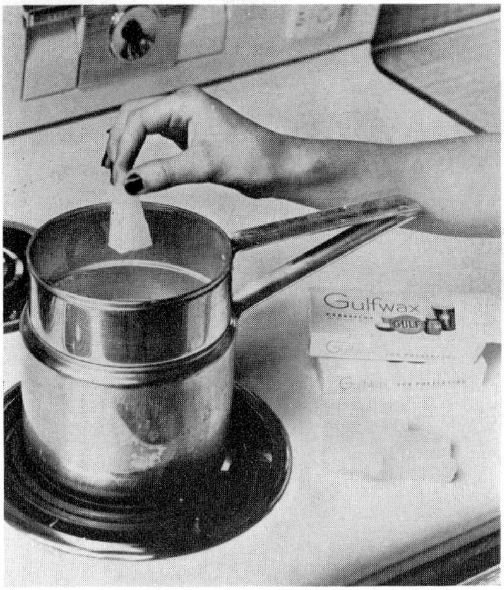

The simple steps in candlemaking: 1. Place the wax in a double boiler.

2. Let it melt completely.

3. Color it with colored crayons. Easy as that and almost as quickly done as told. Photographs courtesy of Gulfwax.

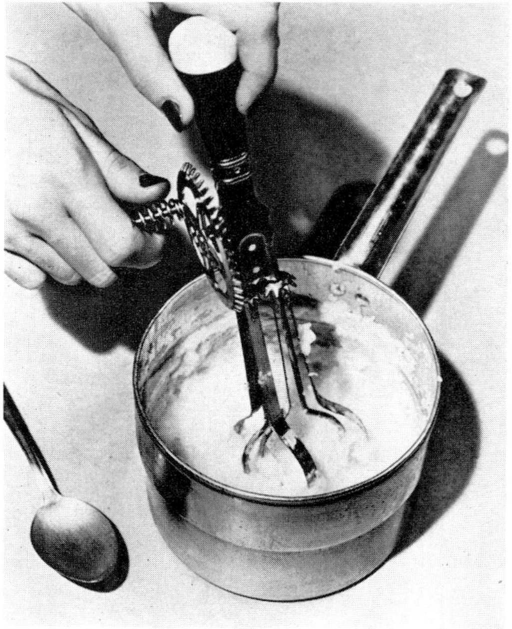

4. Fluffy wax snow, with a twist of the wrist.

5. Beaten with a fork for extra fineness.

6. Fluffy wax snow may be used to make candles—and with that professional touch too.

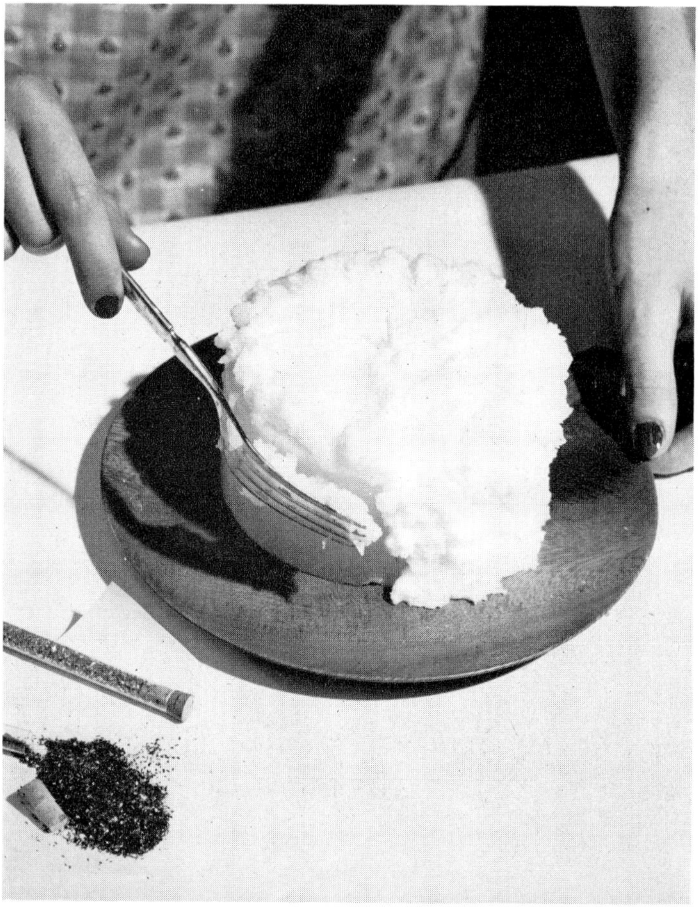

7. Or it may be used to decorate them. Photographs courtesy of Gulfwax.

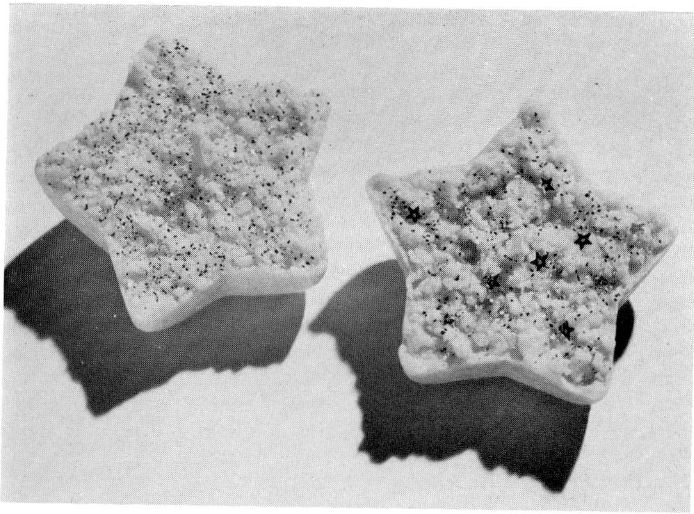

8. and 9. A little wax, a little glitter, a little time. Two attractive examples of candles to try when you are young in candlecraft. At the top: Stars made of wax snow. At the bottom: A birthday-cake candle. Both the birthday candles and the cake candle burn merrily. Photographs courtesy of Gulfwax.

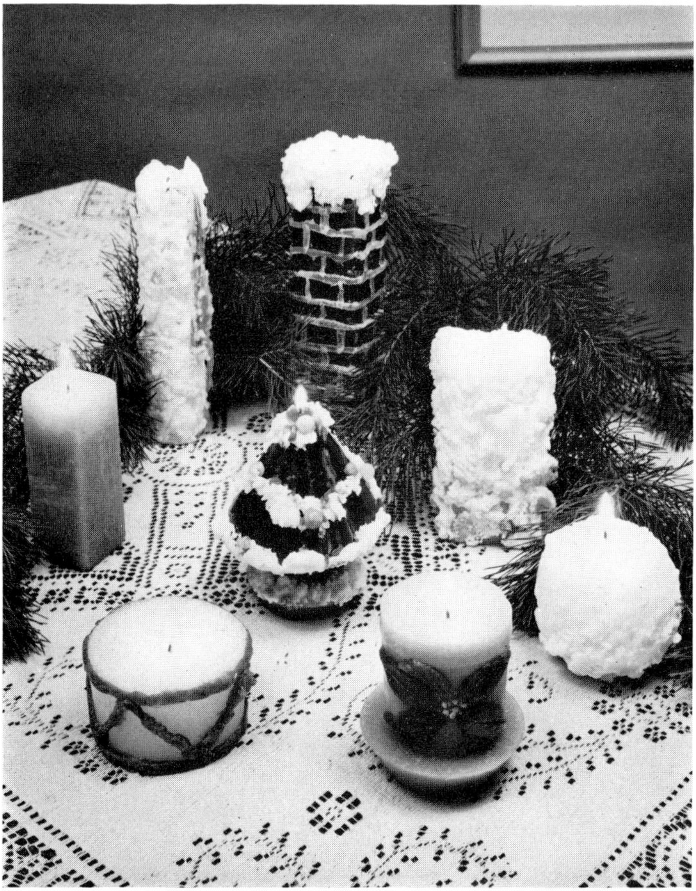

10. Homemade candles for the Christmas season—all easy to do; accomplished with fun and without fuss. Photograph courtesy of Gulfwax.

11. Sealing wax poinsettia on a tall taper by Alice Jaffe. Other candles decorated by Frederick-Thomas. Sequin and glitter on a star pillar; dried flowers on a square pillar candle; sequined mobile design; Christmas wreath and stars, sequined snowball, jewel-studded cone; pearl-decorated black candle. All but the poinsettia taper and star pillar candle are homemade by Michael Powers.

12. Pink and silver waxed flowers on a pillar candle, sealing wax flowers on a taper; jeweled bands on a pillar candle. White reinforcement rings and seals decorate a patio candle. Christmas decorations embellish a homemade cone candle. To the right, a well-burning candle made in a cottage cheese container. In the foreground, wax medallions for floating candles or to decorate pillar candles. A short taper decorated with miniature fruit. A pillar candle enlivened with Christmas bells.

Finish the base of the candle with a close-ranking double row of sequins.

Select a heavy rope candle: Run a row of sequins down each spiral ridge. Or on an Emkay Twisted Pillar Candle —which has a single, deeply-grooved twist—run a row of small sequins in the groove. Space them close together at the base, more widely at the top.

Do corner decorations in sequins: Obviously you will need a square candle. Cluster sequins at the base, and around and up *one* corner, the decoration growing narrower, and the sequins fewer, toward the top. Looks rather like a peaked snowdrift of jewels along one edge of your candle. Only two sides, of course, are decorated.

Sequin icicles are fun: Use them on a short, square or round candle that is quite fat. Begin at the top, pinning sequins thickly all around. Then run them down in uneven fashion—like dripping icicles—over the candle.

Festoon with sequins: Use a large, round, squat candle, such as might be made in a coffee can. At intervals of about 2½ inches around the top, place clusters of sequins. From one cluster to the next pin loops of sequins.

Make sequin patterns: Draw or cut out a simple pattern which has clean, well-defined lines—a leaf is a good example. Prick the outline of the design on the candle. Fill it in with sequins. You may wish to add a few extra sequins here and there—but only a few. Let the single design stand out. You can also write names or dates with sequins in this fashion.

Sequin embroidery: This is for the large round or square candle which offers a good working surface. Select one that burns into a well, leaving the outer rim intact, or a tall dripless type which can carry the decoration near the base. With either the design will remain intact.

Let's take a bunch of grapes as a pattern example. Draw it to scale first, and color it—or find one in a magazine which you can copy. The trick lies in the gradation of color in the sequins used, so that you get depth and shading similar to actual embroidery. You will need sequins of various sizes and colors.

Practice first. Start on the table top, laying the sequins out while you work to get the depth and shade you want. They'll slip about, of course, but this kind of practice will cue you for the actual decorating. Or you can practice on a bar of paraffin. It has a good working surface, and it doesn't matter how many times you shift the pins about on it to get a better effect. When you're satisfied with your sequin embroidery, go to work on an actual candle, tracing your design on first with pinpricks, overlapping the sequins to get shading, manipulating the colors as the pattern grows. With the grape design, you may wish to add leaves and tendrils. Tendrils and leaf stems can be made with small pinned-in-place beads or cord.

> *In earlier days—very, very early days indeed—when candles were in their infancy, they were not done up in fancy dress, but they came in oversized packages. Some of those early candles weighed as much as 300 pounds, which is quite a lot of candle.*

MOBILE DESIGNS. This method of decorating is as amusing as it is engaging. The little mobiles are made from copper wire, embellished with beads, sequins, rhinestones—or whatever you happen to wish to use. A number of them are made, and they are then stuck into the candle as you desire them. The mobiles can be simple or complex, and can be used on almost any type of candle.

Strictly speaking, of course, a mobile is an artistic device in which objects of pleasing shape and form—but not necessarily related—are suspended in a given arrangement. When the mobile is actually in motion, the suspended objects create a constantly changing pattern which is

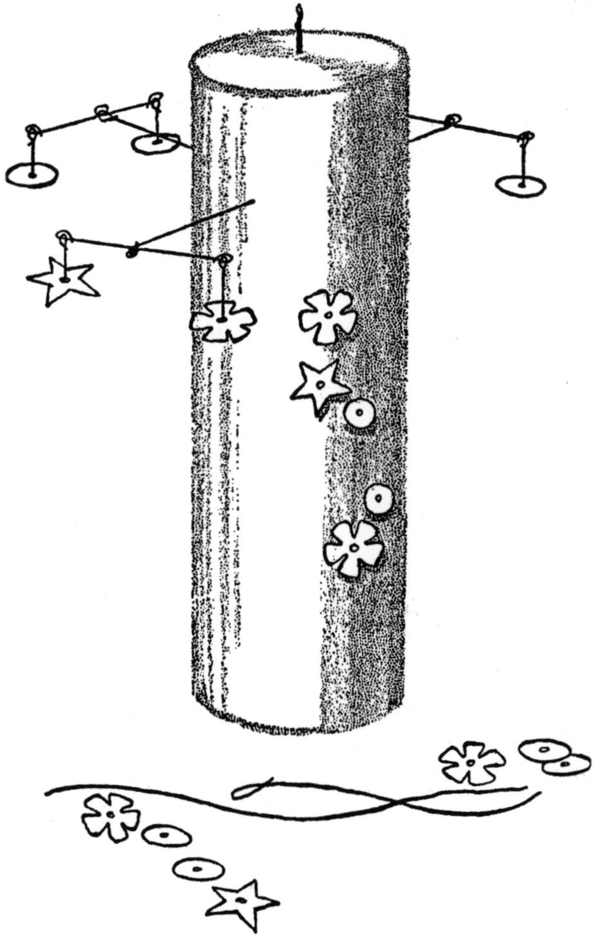

pleasing to the eye. You may want to design, yourself, such art forms for your candles. But if you'd like to follow the spirit of the mobile decoration without the letter of the artistic law, you might try such ideas as the following.

For instance, a simple loop-with-dangle mobile. Cut a piece of copper wire about 3 inches long. Bend one end of it into a loop. Take a second shorter piece of wire. Make a tiny hook in one end of it and then thread on a bead or two, sequins, or whatever you like (the hook keeps them from sliding off). Attach this dangle to the loop in the first wire simply by bending the undecorated end of the short wire in a little hook over the wire loop you first made. Don't tighten this hook so that the dangle is rigid. It should be loose enough so that the dangle swings free from the loop—earring fashion. Make a number of these, of course, and you might run them in a circle around a globe candle. Or you might like them around the top rim of a well-burning candle. Wherever used, they're placed by sticking the straight end of the looped wire into the wax.

You can make simple T mobiles merely by using wire to form a T with the cross bar not rigid. To do this make a small loop in the top of the wire which will act as the upright part of the T. The cross wire is put through this, and kept from sliding by looping it around the first loop you made. Leave enough leeway so that the cross bar will teeter back and forth. Beads, sequins or other decorations are attached to the ends of the cross bar. Stick the end of the upright part of the T into the wax.

Variation on a theme: T mobiles with double or triple cross bars can be made in the same way. Follow the preceding directions, but make additional loops on the upright wire of the T for additional cross bars.

Any kind of free-swinging dangle which you like can be fashioned from wire and decorated with beads, rhinestones, tiny charms, small shells, or whatever decorative material you wish to use.

Spiral Mobile: This is for decorating a slender taper, and is made from fairly heavy copper wire. Cut the wire 2 to 3 inches longer than the taper. Curve it in a gentle spiral which will curl around the taper, but will not touch it. To fasten the spiral in place, wind the lower end of the wire firmly around the base of the taper several times (leave enough candle below to go into the candleholder). The top of the spiral should end 2 inches or so below the top of the candle, so if necessary clip it to size after it has been put in place.

You can, if you like, glue a few sequins or brilliants along the wire, or you could spread it with glue and cover with glitter.

SHELL DECORATIONS. Two of the most handsomely decorated candles I ever saw were in an exclusive Fifth Avenue shop in New York City—and were appropriately priced! I did not buy them for the obvious reason—but I did study them long enough to borrow the idea of their decoration, and I trust I am forgiven for any unlicensed pilfering.

The candles were a beautiful green-blue, clear and with a translucent quality. They were square—about the size of a milk carton, but a little taller. The decoration was fashioned largely from shells—some so tiny and delicate that you could scarcely imagine any little sea animal living in them. Some larger. The largest about the size of giant shell macaroni (which is not particularly poetic, but is graphic).

The shells were clustered thickly around two sides of the candles, at the base—not just set in rows, but glued, one to another, sometimes overlapping, sometimes on top of each other. As the pattern of shells was built up at the corner of the candles (to a height of about 6 inches), it narrowed and grew lighter in feeling, until with a few scattered shells it drifted away.

Here and there among the shells were bits of coral, tiny pearl beads, sometimes a soft-colored stone such as you buy for an aquarium. The candles were, as I said, uniquely lovely. There can be no exact directions for such decorations—you must simply work the shells and pearls and bits of pastel stone into a still-life group which pleases you.

The technique of building the design is quite simple: Shells which are fastened directly to the candle are done so with melted wax (the back of the shell can be dipped, or the wax can be spooned on). The shell is then pressed firmly into place, and held until the wax hardens. If you wish a shell to be somewhat embedded in the candle, use a very sharp knife and carve out a little hole for it to fit into. Shells, pearls, or stones which are fastened to other shells are glued on. This may sometimes mean that one end of a shell may be dipped in wax to fasten to the candle, the other end coated with glue to attach to another shell.

You can lay out a general pattern on a table before you begin to work on the candle itself. If you don't do this, do have well in mind the design you wish to execute. It must grow as you work, so work carefully. Test the position of each shell or other piece of decoration by holding it in place with tweezers before gluing or waxing it down. Once it is fastened in place, it cannot be changed.

Be sure to finish all the base work before you add the top decorations. Such designing as this takes skill, and is not quickly done. But the results are well worth the effort. And if you make a handsome pair of such candles, I can tell you that you will be saving very close to half a hundred dollars!

Incidentally, if you have difficulty in getting sea shells, write to the McArthur Shop, 144 East 61st Street, New York City, 21. Mention this book—and ask for prices or say how much you want to spend.

DESIGNS WITH SEALING WAX. In a charming house in Stamford, Connecticut, a pretty young woman named Alice Jaffe keeps her home, and builds a side-line career as candle decorator. Candle decorating could be a full-time career for Mrs. Jaffe—any number of people have come knocking on her door with excellent offers meant to entice her into the full-time candle business. But Mrs. Jaffe smiles serenely and shakes her head. Right now her first interests are in her home, her husband, and her two sons. They come first, and she turns down the most lucrative offers without a qualm.

Instead of going "strictly commercial," Alice Jaffe maintains her own home business, holding it to the limits of her leisure time, managing it with astuteness and artistic talent—but never letting it encroach on her Number One career—which is homemaking.

I talked to Mrs. Jaffe in New York—she had come down from Stamford one very hot midsummer morning, and she had brought a number of examples of her art—handsome, lovely, and engaging candles which she had decorated. She talked generously of her methods of doing them.

Alice Jaffe's most unique contribution to candle decorating is the use of sealing wax. She now imports her sealing wax, seeking unusual colors and shades—but she began with a simple sealing-wax set such as you might find in almost any stationery store. She advises others to start with such available wax. If your candlemaking turns into a career, then you may wish to explore the greater variety of colors available in imported sealing wax.

Mrs. Jaffe began her career from a card table set in the corner of her dining room. An alcohol lamp, a set of sealing wax, candles in pleasing proportions—these were her basic materials. She had one rule: Never leave the lamp burning and the slim fingers of sealing wax within reach of children who might try to imitate her—and could be badly burned.

Suppose you wish to begin your sealing-wax decoration with swirls of color blended along the length of the taper. The sealing wax is melted over the alcohol flame—just as it would be if you were about to seal a letter. When it is molten, it is spread with swift, sure strokes along the candle. Colors can be blended. Smoky shades are achieved by letting the wax smoke in the flame, and this gives a subtle and interesting effect, more pleasing than straight combinations of harsher colors.

To start the wax on the candle—whether it is for a swirl, a flower, a figure, or written message, you must first place a small dot of the sealing wax on the candle wax. This acts as an anchor for whatever sealing-wax stroke follows. Without that little dot, which drops and embeds itself in the wax, you'll not be able to complete the stroke. Each new stroke on the wax begins with this.

There is almost no limit to the wax decorations you may paint on a candle. The sealing wax is used much as you would use oil paints. Don't worry about what happens when the candle burns. The sealing wax simply melts, like the candle wax. As a matter of fact, it may even be collected from around the flame after the candle has been blown out and the wax cooled.

Mrs. Jaffe's candles do not, of course, stop at the simple —but effective—swirls of color, which are rather similar to the decorations we used to put on every interesting bottle or jar we could lay hands on! One of her cleverest designing ideas is to make tagboard (or similar stiff but manageable paper) cutouts, coat them with sealing wax, and then attach them toward the base of the candles. Suppose, for instance, she wishes to decorate a candle with a petalled flower and green leaves. She cuts the flower and leaves from the cardboard. She then cuts or "paints" each with her sealing wax—coloring both sides, blending her colors to get depth and shading, curling or bending the leaves before the wax is set to give them a realistic look. Details, such as the veins of leaves, are painted on in darker shades of the wax. Flower and leaves are then assembled into a whole, and stuck together with the wax. This is sealed to the candle. You have a three-dimensional decoration. Obviously, the design can be chosen to fit the occasion.

One amusing set of candles was used in the table decorations for a Cub Scout Troop dinner. She cut the Scout figure about 5 inches tall from cardboard, and "painted" it realistically with her sealing-wax colors—including the Troop number. It was a perfect miniature of a Scout. The figure was then sealed (with sealing wax) to the base of the candle. When the candles were placed on the table, there was a row of smartly turned out Cub Scouts. This idea could be adapted for any figure you wished to make.

Sealing-wax decorations, no matter how delicate they

look, are practically indestructible. They pack well, so are good for gifts which must be mailed. They can be re-used —when one candle has been burned down to the decoration, remove it and attach it to a fresh candle if you wish.

You may paint designs directly on candles with sealing wax (remember the beginning dot). Flowers, leaves, monograms—whatever you like. There is only one way to perfect this work—practice. Try for clean, sure strokes, which give a professional look. Practice on candle stubs first, or for that matter, on the side of a jar. Unless you have a very sure sense of design and color, plan both ahead of work. Combinations can be selected to harmonize with a room or table setting.

Mrs. Jaffe also creates smart flower and fruit decorations for candles. For fall, she may select pale-green swirl candles, which have the feeling, if not the actual look, of cornucopias. Toward the center of the candle, she may place a cluster of fruit—miniature apples, pears, bananas, a few leaves—purchased, quite possibly, at the millinery counter of a dime store.

A second candle may have at the base a fat wreath of garden vegetables. A third may be ringed at the base with delicately shaded spring flowers. (These wreaths actually make the candleholders.) A fourth candle may be fashioned of fall leaves and berries, or of evergreens, holly, and pine cones.

These materials are wired together—manipulated to the desired effect as in the making of a corsage—and, generally speaking, they are waxed beforehand. (On page 75, we tell you about waxing flowers.)

One more tip from Alice Jaffe: For artificial flowers, go to the millinery district. Ask for decorations which have faded. Merchants may be surprised—but her artistic reasoning is sound. Faded decorations have softer, more subtle colors. They give the shading which is needed, add charm to the finished work.

ATTIC ACTION. That last note may well send you delving into attic trunks or—barring attics in this modern age, alas!—to digging through boxes where castoff bonnets accumulate. Clip off the flowers, fruits, and vegetable produce. Separate the clusters of flowers. Discard those which are crushed. Dry-clean those which may need it. (And let them air long and thoroughly before getting them near hot wax.) Artificial fruits and vegetables may usually be washed with detergents. Save ornaments, too. They're always useful. And ask your friends for castoff hat trimmings. Let me add that you do not use only the older trimmings. Combine them with brighter, newer ones—as you desire.

WAXING ARTIFICIAL FLOWERS. Flowers to be used in candle decorations, whether they are homemade ones of crepe paper or purchased artificial ones, should be waxed. The process is not complex, but it must be done with care.

Flowers are dipped singly, no matter how small. Trying to do them in clusters—speedy as the idea may seem—will simply result in a wax-works mess.

Melt paraffin in a double boiler or over a pan of hot water. Paraffin should be very hot for the dipping operation (this makes it more liquid), so keep the pan over low heat. Have ready a number of flower holders—pinholders or others—with plenty of newspaper spread under them, and also around your work space. You'll want enough holders so that each flower may be placed separately, not touching any other.

Dip a flower into the hot wax. If petaled like a daisy, simply dip it in and out. If it is a rose type, turn it gently in the wax so that the heart of the flower will be well covered. (No need to dip the wire stems in, by the way.) When you remove the flower from the wax, shake it gently and tap the stem to remove excess and keep drops from forming along the petal edges. (Here, quite obviously, is one reason for the copious use of newspapers.) After flowers stand in the holder, wax drops may still collect. You can remove them with a touch of a toothpick or Q-Tip before they harden.

If you are dipping *paper* flowers, wax from the first dipping will probably be absorbed by the paper. Let flowers dry about 15 minutes, then dip again—exactly the same way. After another 15 minutes, dip a third time if necessary. Artificial fabric flowers may need only one extra dipping. This will depend on the material from which they are made, and on how much of the first dipping is absorbed.

After each dipping, when wax has solidified somewhat but before it has hardened, you may wish to shape the flower petals—give a pleasing curve to daisy petals, for instance, or a slight curl to a leaf, particularly if they are of crepe paper. Mold with your fingers—or a tablespoon may help. Work gently and quickly.

WAX FLOWERS WITH CANDLES. Besides wreaths of flowers which are formed into candleholders, and clusters attached low on a candle, here are some suggestions.

Small single flowers: Such as violets, say. Remove the wire stems. With a bit of melted wax, attach single flowers in a random way over the lower third of a taper, with perhaps two or three flowers reaching above that point. Don't let them run too high on the candle, however, for the candle should only be permitted to burn down to the point where the flowers begin. Otherwise a slight conflagration.

Other small-flower decorations: Use the same technique, to stud the outside of a large round or square candle which burns with a well. Cluster flowers on the outside of a snowball candle. Run them in rows around the base of pillar candles. Let them follow the curve of a rope or twist candle part way up. Or use the single flowers with pearls, tiny shells, or sequins.

Large single flowers: A rose, for instance, and a leaf or two, can be attractive at the base of a pillar candle. You can embellish these by embedding a pearl or two, a very few sequins or rhinestones in the last coating of wax on the petals before it has hardened. Or sprinkle with glitter while the wax is still soft. You can do a bit of design on the candle itself as a frame or background for your flower—glitter in an uneven pattern, jewels, beads, or whatever. This will help tie candle and flower together—designwise that is.

And sometimes with a pair of slender candles, try using the full-blown rose near the base of one, a rose bud with leaves twined around the base of the other.

Sprays of flowers: Bluebells would be an example. They are attractive when waxed to the base of a candle, with a leaf or two added. You may want to fasten one or two of the flowers right on the candle, too, to hold them in a particular place, but by and large the flowers should be free. Single stalks may be spiraled around the lower part of a candle, and waxed into place.

GRASSES, GRAINS, and LEAVES. These may be waxed in the same way as artificial flowers and used for decorations. You might, for instance, place a row of waxed, ripened heads of wheat around the base of a deep-toned candle. Above them, in sunburst effect, embed single grains of wheat. These materials may also be used in forming wreaths and corsages which include flowers.

PRESSED FLOWERS. Use these on larger candles which burn with a well, leaving the sides standing. Select the flowers with an eye to the candle you wish to decorate. Press them in a heavy book, with a sheet of foil under and over them. Arrange flowers and leaves carefully before pressing so that when dried they will be graceful. And let them dry well. When the time comes to use them on the candle, lay them in place, and cover with a piece of waxed paper. Run a hot iron over all. Keep the iron moving, or you'll have dents in the candle.

PRESSED FERNS AND GRASSES. Handle the same way. Dry the grasses so that they won't all have a straight-up-and-down look. Arrange them one by one on the candle, but do the ironing after they are all in place. A square candle is easier to work with than a round one, but if you are patient, a round one can be used. Then grasses must be pressed on in sections.

WAX MEDALLIONS. These are easily made, and handsome on heavier candles. For molds, use individual salad molds, coasters, or any small shallow container which has either an attractive shape, as a star, or a pleasing embossed or engraved design.

Suppose you choose leaf-shaped, plastic coasters from

the dime store. The embossed design of leaf veins gives a clear, interesting pattern. Just oil the coasters and fill them with melted wax of whatever color you like—the same color as the candle, a varying shade of the same color, or a contrasting color. These medallions will be used on a large square candle. Make four of them. Let them harden. Then fasten them to the candles with melted wax—one medallion to each side of the candle.

It is difficult to apply medallions to a round candle. It can be done by letting the medallion set *but not harden.* Dip the mold in hot water to loosen the medallion. Remove it, and handling gently, fasten it to the candle with melted wax, curving it to fit the candle as you do so. The trick is to unmold the medallion at a time when the wax will hold its shape, but you can still bend it as required.

A word about monogrammed coasters—which a good many people turn to automatically. You can't form your medallion by pouring the wax *into* the coaster. If you do, your letters are reversed when you take the mold out. You can, if a single letter is indented on the underside of the coaster, make a thin medallion here, and the letter will come out right. Handle with care though—such medallions are very fragile.

RAINBOW CANDLES. These are quick to do and offer a fine way to entertain a youngster on a rainy day. For this purpose get the short, inexpensive "household" candles.

You need a pan of warm water, and oil paints of several harmonizing colors. Drop a little of each onto the surface of the water—each color in a separate place. Don't stir, let the colors spread by themselves. Then dip a candle in and pull it out with a twirling motion. Let it dry. If you used a candle taller than the pan, dip just one half, let it dry, then dip the other half.

PATIO CANDLES. Don't miss the fun of decorating these. You know them, of course—the candles which come in glass, should I say, chimneys or jackets? There are short ones and tall ones, and they all offer scope for decoration.

Avis Stendal of New York (some of her clever gift packaging appears in *Gifts from Your Kitchen,* M. Barrows & Company, Inc., New York) presents a group of ideas for decorating these candles. I think you'll like them.

Part of the charm of these candles comes when the flame shows through the glass and illuminates your design. So don't make the design too solid—unless you use paints or paper through which the design will show. Then you will have a stained-glass window effect—and more about that soon.

Calico candles: Make a design with gummed dots, seals, and paper-reinforcement rings found at stationery counters. Or use pieces from children's paste-up games. Because the gum is apt not to stick on glass, apply the decorations with rubber cement.

Use narrow gold braid, rubber-cemented in barber-pole fashion around the glass. Finish the top with a band of slightly wider braid.

Monogrammed candles: You might cut out Old English letters from an advertisement. You might buy the gold and silver letters which come in sheets. You might cut your own from metallic paper. Apply any of these with rubber cement. Frame the monogram with narrow braid, paper beading, or passe partout.

Fairyland candle: Clip patterns and medallions from a silver-paper doily. Rubber-cement them over the glass in a delicate tracery design. Here and there—but sparingly—rubber-cement a shining sequin, and you will have an ever-changing succession of shadow pictures on your table as the candle burns.

Sequins and beads: They are as effective on the glass as when applied directly to the candle. Try a design with clusters close to the base of the candle container, but arranged more sparingly toward the top. Remember that sequins and beads are not transparent, so don't apply them too thickly.

Frills and fringe: Cut fringe from metallic paper about an inch wide—or a little wider. Curl it with a table knife. Set one band around the top, one around the base of the container. In between, scatter a few sequin stars.

Or you might do a design of painted flowers emerging from a fringe "flower pot." First, with glass paint (or failing this, use enamel), paint delicate stems, leaves, and blossoms directly on the glass. Leave about an inch clear at the base for the flower pot. Make this from three bands of curled metallic fringe, one band glued above another all the way around the glass. For the fringe, use paper which is metallic on *both* sides. Inverted, it flares out from the container to form the rim of the flower pot.

Silky cellophane fringe, sometimes used at Christmas, can also give you a quick-and-easy decoration for a patio candle. Just cut a band of it long enough to go around the glass. Trim it to the proper height. Rubber-cement the band around the top of the glass. Finish with a band of braid or passe partout. Amber and pink fringe look particularly nice.

Color transparencies for decoration: Use these on patio candles if color photography is your hobby. A floral still life or a ring of scenic pictures, set in a frame of passe partout, can be rubber-cemented to encircle the glass. The fun comes when the candle flame illuminates the pictures. Good conversation pieces.

Stained glass effects: One way to get these is to paint on a design with glass paint. Plan it first, unless you are good at freehand drawing. Make a pattern on a piece of paper the same size as the surface of the candle. If the candle is removable, take it out and Scotch-tape your pattern *inside* the glass. Then simply follow this pattern outside as you paint.

If the candle cannot be removed, trace the pattern onto the glass through a fairly heavy carbon paper. Scotch-tape carbon and pattern in place. Then trace slowly and firmly with a hard pencil. Some lines will not come clear, but if you are careful, enough will to serve as a guide. Paint in the colored sections first, and be careful not to carry the color over the carbon tracing lines. And work carefully, so as not to smudge these lines. Let the colored paint dry completely. Then wash the glass to remove the carbon marks. Dry, and paint in the black "leaded" divisions.

Paper cutouts: Metallic papers in all colors are good here. You might, for instance, cut narrow (about ⅛-inch) freehand swirls and rubber-cement them all over the outside of the glass, finishing top and bottom with bands of metallic paper or ornamental paper beading. You might do a spider web (don't fold the paper and do cut with a razor blade). Or do a modern design with squares and cubes and triangles in harmonizing colors. You can cut out amusing stickmen figures, and parade these around the glass. Just let your fancy be your guide.

Jeweled patio candles: Glass stones from dime-store jewelry make elegant decorations with great charm when the candlelight shines through them. A ring of oval or rectangular stones might be set about a third of the way down the glass container, and at about half-inch intervals. Use gold or silver paint to make the "settings." Or form the stones into a medallion on one side of the container, again with the painted-on setting. Or large and small stones of different shapes, sizes and colors might be glued like a studding over the glass.

Or use a single stone in a glittering filigree setting, which will be like a large medallion. Clip it out of a gold- or silver-paper doily, or paint it on the glass with glue and sprinkle with glitter before the glue dries. (Don't try to do the whole medallion before applying the glitter. Work in sections, so that the glue won't dry before the glitter is sprinkled on.) Select glitter in gold or silver, or in a color which harmonizes with the stone. Or apply multi-colored glitter for a sparkling effect. The filigree of the design is best done freehand, or from a pattern Scotch-taped inside the glass.

Glue is, of course, not the easiest thing in the world to paint with. Takes a little patience. Washing the brush in hot water now and then helps.

Flowered patio candles: One trick is to sew heads of small artificial flowers here and there on a piece of net, with perhaps an occasional rhinestone or bead for sparkle. Then sew the net snugly and neatly around the candle container. Finish at top and bottom by gluing on a band of braid.

Lace with an interesting pattern can be used instead of net. Not too many flowers here. They are secondary because of the pattern of the lace.

Artificial flowers can be glued directly on the glass. Daisy heads—each about the size of a silver dollar—look gay in a ring about a third of the way down the container.

Leaf tips or a green band of Mystik Tape can be glued around the base of the container for a finish. Or paint the brown twigs of an apple-blossom branch on the glass with glass paint or oils. Then glue the artificial blossoms in place. Not too many—you might keep a Japanese print in mind as a guide. Vines with stems and tendrils painted on, and artificial leaves glued in place are attractive. Don't glue the leaves flat. Fasten them with just a dot of glue so that they have a free look.

Tailored patio candles: Do these with bands of metallic braid, passe partout, or colored adhesive-backed tape. Run rings of tape at intervals around the glass. Or use vertical strips and glue finishing bands around top and bottom. Metallic rick-rack is interesting for either horizontal or vertical pattern, or in a geometric design. Or try squares, rectangles, and triangles of colored cellophane, glued in a modern pattern to the glass, with neat and narrow gold-braid frames around each shape.

Gold and silver cord: With these, there are many ways to achieve pleasing effects. Select a fine cord, for instance. Apply glue to a length of it. Start at the bottom of the glass container, and go round and round the glass, drawing each row tight against the preceding one. When you have a band as wide as you want—probably about an inch—clip the cord and tuck the end under the top row or two for a neat finish. (A corsage pin will help you. Press down firmly when the tucking-under is finished.) Now cut additional lengths of the cord—anywhere from 3 to 8 inches. Apply glue to them, and fasten them to the sides of the container in swirls and squiggles, just as braid embroidery would be sewed on a dress. Let each piece of cord dry before fastening on to the next. Work neatly to avoid smearing the glass with glue. As a finish, wind rings of cord around the top of the glass, just as you did around the bottom, but only about half an inch deep. The cord gives an interesting embossed look.

Did you know that candles were once the precious property of men of means? They were far beyond a poor man's reach, and it's said that St. Patrick, wishing to remember those who had befriended him, gave rush lights to the poor. These were made of reeds, stripped to the pith at one end, dipped in oil and lighted. They were not as grand as candles, and they smoked as they burned, but to the cottagers who had had nothing but firelight to light their homes, they were a miracle.

NOVELTY CANDLES. This section is the idea mart—suggestions for decorating candles from here, there, and everywhere. Start working with this craft, and you will find yourself on the receiving end of all manner of ideas—which is a wonderful place to be. Friends bring suggestions. It's part of the fun—I suppose part of the fun of most things is in sharing. And in this pleasant business of making and decorating candles, friends seem to share with you two ways: their enjoyment of work you do; their generous giving of ideas for you to use. It's a lively thing, this warm exchange. And, I think, the very core of this book. Which is only as it should be. What good is a book—any book on crafts—if it is merely "how to"? And especially a book on candles which, along with sunsets, and stars and night, and rainbows after summer showers, are among the most friendly things.

Here then are ideas which many friends have contributed. Thanks to each one of them!

COPPER WASHERS. Such as plumbers use, split circles of copper, and rather fanciful. Stud the lower quarter of a pillar candle with them, sealing them in place with melted wax. Even lines if you wish a tailored look. A more random pattern, uneven at the top, for a freer form of decoration.

UPHOLSTERY NAILS. Some have extremely interesting patterns on the heads, and all you need do to apply them is stick them in place. A tufted pattern is interesting. Good on large candles. Use the nails sparingly on slender candles. It's a good idea to heat the nail part—in a candle flame!—and then insert while hot. The nails are a little heavy, and having them heated makes them less apt to crack the wax.

PAPER CLIPS AND BRADS. March a spiral of close-ranked copper paper clips around a large round candle—do a picket-fence of clips and brads around a tall, square candle. Here's how: Begin at the base. Set the clips in groups of three, separated by two brads. Place the first clip so that the bottom touches the base of the candle. The second clip touches the first, but is half an inch higher. The third touches the second, and is even with the first—in short: a picket, with a higher center section.

Now place the two brads, touching the clip and each other. (Actually you don't want to have holes in the fence.) Then make another picket of three paper clips, and continue on around the candle. The second row of "fencing" will be 2½ to 3 inches above the first row. And you may want a third, depending on the height of the candle.

What you have, when you are finished, is not a fence at all, of course, but an interesting geometric pattern.

You might also cover the sides of a squat, square candle (one which burns with a well) with triangles of paper clips —one for each side, one for the base, all corners touching. Work geometrically, and place brads in between to complete the pattern. Something like designing linoleum.

MACARONI DECORATIONS. Use bows, shells, alphabet letters—whatever. Paint them with tempera or oil paint. Spray them with plastic. Fasten them to a candle with melted wax. Either use well-burning candles, or keep the decorations below the burning line. Incidentally, you don't need to discard candles decorated on the lower half or third, even if they can't be burned beyond that point. Decorations can be removed and the stub used for a Memory Candle or melted down to use in other molds.

FISHERMAN'S LUCK. Use fishing flies for the main motif—and on a well-burning candle. Stick them in place with melted wax. Run fine cord from hook to hook in an interesting loop fashion, either pinning or waxing it to the candle.

PINS WITH COLORED HEADS. Not corsage pins. The kind you want are shorter and have round colored heads. They can be worked in any way you like, from spelling out names to geometric patterns, or for making the outlines of flowers. If you can't find such pins, use a short pin, run through a bead. If the hole in the bead is so large that the pin head won't hold, thread a tiny "beading" bead on the pin first. Cut pins to short lengths with wire clippers before placing them.

PAINT DESIGNS WITH COLORED CRAYONS. Plan the design first, and if you need a guide, place your tracing paper over the candle and lightly prick in the outline of the design. To paint with a crayon, melt the tip over a flame (but not to the dripping stage). Draw on the candle while the crayon is soft. Work in short, quick strokes, reheating the crayon briefly, drawing a stroke or two, heating again, and so on. Which is a cue to the kind of picture you can paint—*not* one of fine lines and elaborate design. Practice on a bar of paraffin a few times to see the effects you can create.

FOREIGN TRAVEL. This is for well-burning types—which leave the outer rim of the candle intact. Simply tack labels from foreign resorts and hotels in hit-or-miss fashion around a large candle. Fasten them with small copper nails or pins with colored heads. Spray on a coat of plastic. And this could be college stickers, lodge stickers, convention stickers—or anything similar.

PAINTBOX CANDLES. Collect the little cups in which the colors are set in a paintbox. Wash them, and fill with various colors of wax, leaving the rim of each dish showing. (Fill gently; they overflow in a hurry.) When the wax is hard, seal the cups about 2 inches above the base of a pillar candle. Fasten with melted wax. Or arrange the cups, polka-dot fashion, on the outside of a short, squat candle.

FRIENDSHIP CIRCLE. Remember friendship bracelets: silver links, engraved with the names of friends and relatives? Your bracelet probably began with a single link —worn on a black velvet ribbon—and grew by birthdays.

This candle decoration is simply a borrowing of that idea, and is for a round candle about the circumference of a soup can.

Basic needs: A clean soup can, a pair of tin-cutting shears, enamel or nail polish. Cut your links from the can. Get signatures of friends. Trace them on the tin links. Using a fine brush, paint in the names with enamel or nail polish. Set the links around the candle, using shiny thumbtacks between them.

COINS AND BUTTONS. Some very handsome formal decorations can be done with old coins, held in place with melted wax. You might, for instance, set an interesting coin, medallion-fashion, on one side of a tapered pillar candle. Frame the coin or not, as you wish. . . . Or arrange coins in a circle around a candle. At the base, or in any way that pleases you. Interesting buttons also lend themselves to all manner of decorations—the type of button will help decide the design.

Prognosticator: Did you know that fortunes were once foretold and futures read in the shapes found in the drippings from candles? All manner of things were prophesied: life, death, marriage, prosperity, the inevitable journey. A triangular shape meant success. A tear-shaped drop of wax indicated sorrow. Curves represented false friends. And if you have a fortune-telling book handy, you can probably find all the other mystic signs and meanings. Have a little trouble, though, getting much of a fortune in these days of dripless candles!

I shall light a candle
of understanding in thine heart,
which shall not be put out.

THE APOCRYPHA

III

Special-Day Decorations

HOW TO MAKE UNUSUAL CANDLES FOR CHRISTMAS, EASTER, BIRTHDAYS, WEDDINGS, AND ANNIVERSARIES

ANY DAY IS SPECIAL when candlelight is used, but special days deserve an extra mark of recognition. And candles can be decorated to suit any day, any occasion. Just let the calendar be your cue.

We begin our calendar with Christmas. You know, of course, that the candle which burns in your window at Christmas time follows an old, old tradition—one which dates from the time of Martin Luther. Here is the light to guide the Christ Child, should He visit the earth this night. And its welcome atones for that first Christmas when there was no room at the inn.

Bethlehem, Pennsylvania, is America's Christmas City. Here the old customs of the Moravian Church are still observed. The afternoon before Christmas a trombone serenade from the church steeple ushers in the impressive celebration. At a special service on Christmas Eve, huge trays laden with lighted wax tapers are passed among the congregation while they sing:

Behold, a great, a heavenly light
From Bethlehem's manger shining bright.

The church glows with soft light from hundreds of candles. Many of these are made in Simon Rau's drugstore, the oldest apothecary shop in America. Here the candles are cast of beeswax in molds almost exactly like those of the original Moravian settlers. And these candles add a note of authenticity to the traditional ceremonies.

Faith, Hope, and Charity. In the Roman Catholic Church the burning candle symbolizes these three—Faith to dispel the darkness of unbelief; Hope, which tends toward the possession of the joys of Heaven; Charity, which should burn in our hearts for God and for our neighbor.

There is a particular pleasure in decorating Christmas candles, I think—because they are so beautiful and because their meaning goes so deep. Packages which go from parents' homes to the homes of their children should always include the special Christmas candle. And on Christmas Eve when the two distant candles are lighted, they burn, I believe, with more-than-usual brightness.

In the shops, there is always an exciting collection of Christmas candles—and a wealth of unadorned, inexpensive ones just waiting to be decorated. The holiday season is a happy one for candle craftsmen. And here are some ideas to start you on your way.

GOLDEN GLITTER. Brush white candles quickly with melted wax, or dip them and drain briefly. Sprinkle thickly with golden glitter before the wax hardens. Don't cover the base which goes into the candleholder, and do handle gently. Stand the candles in holders until the wax has completely hardened. All accomplished in a few minutes—and handsome to see.

Glitter postscript: If you are making your own candles, try this: Melt the wax. Color with white crayon. Let the wax cool until it is just "pourable." Add a vial of golden glitter. Pour into an oiled Pilsener glass. Stir. Let cool a little longer. Add a second vial of glitter. Stir until this shows at the sides of the glass. Set in the refrigerator, and, if the glitter settles, continue to stir at frequent intervals. When the wax is completely hard, insert a wick. You have an unusual, cone-shaped candle.

SILVER SPRAY CANDLES. Select red tapers and dip the top third in melted red wax. Stand upright so the wax will run down unevenly (and if it doesn't, drip on a little extra wax quickly). Sprinkle thickly with silver glitter at once. Let dry. Stud the lower two-thirds of the candle with tiny silver-star sequins. This candle is also lovely if the base candle is turquoise (the same color melted wax for the dipping, of course).

GLITTER GLOBES. Make or buy white snowball candles. Stud the rough outer surface with glittering rhinestones which will wink and sparkle in the light. Add a colored sequin here and there. Or you might use just rhinestones, and around the base of the globe, pin a circle of glossy holly leaves and a few berries.

SPANGLE CANDLES. Select rope or twisted candles. For decoration, you will want a goodly number of gold coin-dot paillettes, short pins, and tiny silver beads. Thread a bead onto a pin, then through a paillette. (The bead holds it and adds a bright note too.) Fasten the paillettes in close formation along one twist of the candle, about a third way up. They hang like dangles, and should overlap. If you wish, decorate a second twist, but don't carry the paillettes quite so high this time.

BUGLE-BEAD BEAUTY. Select smooth tapers of whatever height you like. The number of bugle beads you need depends on the height of the taper—but there must be enough to cover thickly about one-third of the taper. On black or white tapers, try varicolored beads, which will give a kaleidoscope of color. Gold beads are handsome on red tapers, and silver on green. Cover the base of the candle—the part which goes into the holder—with adhesive tape. Pour the beads onto a paper, and shake it until they are in close formation. The area covered by the beads should be a little longer than a third of the height of the taper, and a little wider than its circumference.

Now dip the lower third of the candle in melted wax of the same color. Let it drain briefly until the wax is set but not hardened. Then roll the candle gently but firmly across the beads so that they adhere to the newly waxed portion. Stand the candle upside down in a glass to dry. Before peeling off the tape at the base, run a sharp knife around the edge of the tape to cut the wax. Otherwise part of the bead decoration will peel off along with the tape.

To finish the decoration, run a narrow strip of gold, silver, or varicolored metallic braid along the top of the bead decoration, gluing it into place. Leave a small space and run a cord the same color as the braid about ⅛ inch above it.

Variation: Decorate candles in the same fashion using mica snow instead of beads. Have the snow thick before rolling the candle in it.

JINGLE-BELL CANDLES. Tiny gold and silver bells can be used in various ways for Merry Christmas candles. Fasten them to the candles with short snips of wire run through the bell loops bent together, twisted once. Run the ends of the wire into the candle to hold them. Don't leave the ends too long or you'll have trouble poking them into the wax.

You might like a ring of gold bells around a snowball candle. Pin a sparse sprinkling of snowflake sequins here and there.

Or pin four or five bells along each of the ridges of a twisted candle—from the base up, but don't go above the middle of the candle. It can only be burned down to the bells—unless, of course, the bells are taken off, one by one, as the flame goes lower.

A row of bells around the top of a square candle is gay, and a few gold- or silver-star sequins placed on the sides below the bells add to the fun.

A length of copper wire can be swirled around a globe candle. It shouldn't touch the globe, and this is managed either by using paper brads or making wire fasteners—a short length of wire folded over the longer wire, twisted once, the ends poked into the wax. Tie bits of gold cord through the loops on the bells. Glue them to the free-form swirl which twists around the globe.

Make graduated rings of wires with bells attached and

slip them onto a taper. You will probably want about five rings for a tall candle, not more than three for a short one. Two or three bells per ring is all you want. Carefully measure the wire for the rings so they will fit at even distances up the lower third or so of the candle. Twist the wire ends neatly together for a finished look. Wire the bells to these rings. And remember—the largest ring goes into place first.

> *Bell By-Line: These bell designs can be adapted for New Year's, weddings, anniversaries. The color of the candle used makes the difference.*

CHRISTMAS CORSAGE CANDLES. A number of attractive corsages can be made for various kinds of candles—tall slim tapers, rope candles, heavy square or round ones, pillar candles—any kind. The operation consists of fashioning a pretty corsage—or buying one, for that matter—and fastening it near the base of the candle. The size and general shape of the corsage should fit the type of candle.

It's more fun to make your own corsages than to buy them. Holly, Christmas greens, bright berries, small colored Christmas-tree balls or similar tree decorations, ribbons, and tinsel are wired together, and either tied or wired to the candle. Do remember to keep the corsage near the base of the candle—and don't let the candle burn down low enough to run the risk of lighting the evergreen sprigs or ribbons. Here are a few corsage ideas which you may like:

Wreath corsages for the base of tapers. A wide wreath if the taper is very tall, a narrow one if short. Make the wreath in a ring to fit the base of the candle, just above the holder. Glossy holly leaves, bright red berries, a few silver leaves, and a red ribbon bow make a handsome wreath. . . . Or use long-needled pine for the frame of the wreath, wiring together small pieces so that all the needles point in the same direction and are thickly set. To this frame, wire clusters of tiny Christmas-tree balls. Small gilded pine cones would also be attractive.

Poinsettia and green leaves, but not a wreath corsage. Use artificial leaves and flower. Fashion them into a corsage. Use on a white candle, or at any rate, not on a red one for red of candle and red of poinsettia are apt to clash. Incidentally, Alice Jaffe, whom we have mentioned before, makes poinsettias and leaves from limber cardboard and coats them with sealing wax.

Gilt and silver grain: You can buy artificial grains, or gild and silver your own. Wire them together, cat's-whisker fashion. At the center, wire a cluster of foil-covered nuts. (In order to fasten foil-covered items in place, leave a small twist of the foil, to which attach a wire. With this, you can fasten them to the corsage.)

Mistletoe spiral: Cover a wire with florist's green tape, leaving about ½ inch top and bottom, uncovered. To this wire fasten—thickly, please—bits of mistletoe. Add a few bright berries or tiny colored balls—the size which come strung like beads to drape on a tree. Push one end of the wire into the candle just above the base. Gently spiral the wire around the candle, to about a third of the way up. Then bend the other end and poke it into the candle. These spirals are rather nice on rope candles. Let the mistletoe spiral follow the candle twist.

Sequined holly: Wire glossy holly leaves (but no berries) together to make the base of a corsage. At the center, wire a cluster of red and silver Christmas-tree balls—small but of different sizes. Now wire corsage to candle and glue a few sequins to the holly leaves. Pin a sparse drift of sequins to the candle above the corsage.

Corsage stars: For the base of your corsage, select a small star-shaped reflector, the kind used on tree lights. Between star points at the top, wire a few delicate sprays of long, silvered pine needles. Cluster Christmas balls and a few more silvered pine needles at the center. For extra glamour, instead of silvering the needles, brush with glue and sprinkle with glitter.

Glitter leaves: Brush green leaves with glue and sprinkle with glitter. Use these as the base of the corsage. Wire a cluster of Christmas balls at the center.

Trumpet corsage: Use bits of evergreens and loops of red ribbon for the base. Wire on a tiny gold trumpet—dime-store type. Cut tiny musical notes from gold paper —eighths, triplets, sixteenths. (Use a razor blade—they're awfully tiny, I know, and you'll cut the tops off six before you get one good one!) Fasten them to the candle with dots of melted wax—just above the corsage, and sprinkled up toward the center of the candle.

Red rose: Use bits of evergreen for the base, and a bright-red, full-blown rose for the center—an artificial one. Glue one or two rhinestones to the petals. Tie in place with a matching red ribbon.

Starlight: This is fun, and very gay. Begin by wiring six or eight pipe cleaners together at the center. If you are decorating a tall taper, snip these so they'll be shorter. Bend them to form a pompon. Brush each with glue and cover with gold glitter. When they are dry, glue a twinkling array of silver-star sequins to the cleaners—one at each end of each cleaner, a few others here and there along their lengths. Work carefully—tweezers will help—you don't want to bend the pompon, knock off the glitter, or dislodge the stars.

To set off the pompon, make a round base by wiring evergreens together. Paint or spray it with ice-blue color. Wire it carefully to the back of your star pompon. Then wire or tie to the candle—a silver ribbon, please. It's a rather handsome affair.

Postscript: Tiny pompons can also be made of wire instead of pipe cleaners, with gold lace-paper doilies, cut to size, for the backing. They can be pinned to the candles.

Added items: There's no limit to the type of corsage you can make for a Christmas candle. Try gilding or silvering a few sea shells of varying shapes and sizes; blue on a pearl here, a sequin there. Glue the finished shells to a glitter-sprayed twig of a shape to suggest a corsage. Tie or wire the finished product to your candle.

For a large, square candle, glue into a small, star-shaped gelatin mold a little heap of Christmas-tree ornaments of different kinds: toy trumpets, stars, all such. Glue each into place—and it's wise to visualize the finished product before gluing, which is so final! Back the star-mold with holly leaves or other greens. Tie the corsage into place by running a gold or silver cord over all and around the candle; or use melted wax.

One more idea: Cut three stars from cardboard—big, medium, and small, like the Three Bears; determine their sizes by the candle which they will adorn. Gild them, and deck with a few sequins. Remove the stem from an artificial rose. Drive a glitter-topped corsage pin through the center of the rose, and through the center of the smallest star. Then run the pin through a ⅛-inch bead. Now drive the pin through the center of the middle-sized star, through another bead, and the third star. Finally fasten your corsage to your candle, with the corsage pin.

> ◆§ *Christmas Special: The Puritans made Christmas candles primed with a bit of gunpowder. They were timed and lighted so that Christmas was ushered in with a flash of light—and a giant firecracker explosion.*

GOLDEN-BAUBLE CANDLE. Select a short, heavy, round or square candle—creamy-white or black would be handsome. Run a band of gold metallic braid around top and bottom. (It can be pinned on.) Stud the sides—not too thickly—with gold Christmas balls, the 1-inch size. Fasten on the ornaments with inch-long pieces of wire. Put a wire through the loop at the top of each ball, bend the wire double, twist it once, and then stick the ends of the wire into the candle. The balls can be placed in a quilting pattern, in deep scallops, or in any other pattern you like. Arranging balls in circles on the sides of a square candle is interesting. Use a cutout paper circle as a guide.

COOKY-CUTTER CAPER. You'll want a square candle about the size of a quart milk carton. (Some you buy are slightly tapered, but that's all right.) Melt ¼ pound of paraffin and color with a green crayon. Pour a ¼-inch layer into a pan. When the wax is set, but not hard, cut out four Christmas trees with a cooky cutter of proper shape. (And you may need a sharp knife to help cut the edges clean.) Remove the trees carefully—a spatula will help. Cover the backs with melted wax to fasten them to the candle, one to a side, and about ½ inch from the base of the candle. Press the trees firmly into place and let dry.

For a ground line, run a length of heavy green cord around the candle just below the trees. Pin the cord in place or wax it to the candle.

Then decorate the four trees. You can tip the branches with bright sequins; festoon them with lines of tiny gold and silver beads, or use small bells at the tips of the tree branches. Festoons of red and white beads, alternated, will look like old-fashioned popcorn-and-cranberry strings. A very gay look can be achieved by pinning bits of tinsel to the tips of the branches.

Did you know that in England it was once the custom for village children to present the schoolmaster with candles on the last day of the term before Christmas? No gift could have been more welcome, for this honored gentleman's pay scarcely covered such luxuries.

CHRISTMAS TREES. You can make your own by coloring melted wax with green crayons, and using a greased Pilsener glass for the mold. Let the wax cool somewhat before pouring it into the glass—always safe procedure when using a glass mold. When the candle is hard, mount it on a small spool (painted brown) for the base—it can be attached with hot melted wax.

Festoon the trees with lines of glittering sequins. . . . Attach tiny balls. . . . Fasten on bits of tinsel. . . . Use bright beads. An all-white tree with blue-and-silver trimming is pretty. Or a pink tree with gold.

You can, of course, buy molded Christmas-tree candles and trim them yourself. Some candles come with wax decorations already drawn on them. If you prefer to make your own, simply dip the tree in melted green wax once or twice. Let it harden. And then proceed at will.

CHRISTMAS PATIO CANDLES. Stained-glass-window effects (described in Chapter 2) are nice. You might do these in a simplified nativity scene, for instance, tracing your design onto black paper, cutting it out with a razor blade, pasting the cellophane or tissue in place to give the desired color effect. Craft and art books usually include such scenes which can be copied if you do not trust your own drawing.

Snowflakes clipped from gold or silver paper and glued to the glass of a patio candle make an attractive design. . . . Bands of tinsel glued around the glass are gay and sparkling. . . . Sequins can be used to advantage. . . . You can fasten tree decorations to the glass with dots of glue right on the ornaments, or tie small ribbon bows through the loops on the decorations, and then glue these to the glass. . . . Lettering—Noel, Merry Christmas, or a greeting—can be written on with glass paint, or you can purchase gold and silver letters and rubber-cement them to the glass. . . . Figures or designs can be cut from Christmas cards and rubber-cemented to the glass—perhaps a ring of them around top and bottom, perhaps figures centered on one side.

CHRISTMAS SNOWMEN. You will need three snowball candles, or candle globes (see Chapter 1 if you wish to make them), a small one, a medium-sized one, a large one. Fasten them together with melted wax—in proper snowman fashion. When this wax has hardened, draw eyes, nose, and mouth on the head, using colored crayons, the tips slightly melted in a candle flame. Don't let the crayons melt too much or they will run when you try to draw. Sequins or bright beads make gay buttons down the snowman's jacket—that is to say, on the middle-sized snowball candle.

CHIMNEY CANDLES. (See Illustration 10.) You will need a square, red candle—either bought or made. Groove the wax on the sides to represent bricks. An ice pick makes a good "groover," and you will need a ruler, preferably with a metal edge, to use as a guide when drawing the straight lines. Your masonry must not look shaky. Make the grooves reasonably deep. Just brush off the little curls of wax which will appear. Melt some white wax and beat it into snow, as described in Chapter 1. Pile this around the top of the chimney. Incidentally, a white candle which is coated with red will add interest to your brickwork, for as you groove the candle, the white will show through and emphasize the lines of the bricks. If you can't buy such a candle, you could get a white one the right size and shape, and dip it in red. Or for that matter, you could get a red candle and dip it in white. The effect will be just as good.

> *Early Item: They say that King Arthur of York kept the first Christmas feast—back in* A.D. *521. And they say, too, that this feast, noble in proportion, was lighted by hundreds of flickering candles.*

CHRISTMAS DRUM CANDLE. (See Illustration 10.) For this you need a short, round candle—drum-shaped, in other words. Red or green for the color. Melt a little white wax and pour it into a flat pan to a thickness of about ⅛ inch. When the wax is set, but before it is hard, cut strips of the desired width for decoration—probably a little wider than ⅛ inch, but that depends on the size of the candle. Run the strips zigzag from top to bottom around the sides of the candle—and better measure your distances first so you will come out even. Press the strips firmly in place so they will stick. If they have set a little too much, some melted wax dripped on the back will make them stick. Finish the drum by running a strip of the white wax around top and bottom.

> *Did you know that in olden times good folk believed there was only one night of the year when evil spirits might be discussed with safety? And this was on Christmas Eve when the lighted candles burned bright and clear.*

CHRISTMAS RIBBON CANDLES. Take a tall slender candle, and spiral a strip or strips of wax around it. Make these by pouring melted wax of the desired color into a square cake pan to a depth of about ¼ inch. Before this wax is hard, cut it into ½-inch strips, and spiral them around the taper, working from the bottom up, and pressing the lower side of the strip firmly against the candle, letting the upper edge flare out a little. You can use any number of interesting color combinations. You might, for instance, run green or red strips around a white candle, gold around green, silver around red. You might sprinkle glitter on the spiraled strips before they harden.

SNOW CANDLES. Select candles of any type to decorate with wax snow, made as described in Chapter 1. You can cover the outside of a pillar candle; run a rim of snow around the edges of a square candle; festoon a cone-shaped candle; cover tall slim candles and sprinkle them with glitter before the snow has hardened. With wax snow, you can form a snowball around the base of a tall candle. All these snow trimmings are easy to do, and most effective. Just remember not to apply the snow too hot. It tends to slide off if it hasn't cooled a bit.

How many other Christmas candles are there? As many as there are candle craftsmen making them, as many as there are ideas which spring from the yuletide season. And who is to say how many this may be? They range from a bright gaiety to solemn beauty. May they all burn serenely and with a peaceful loveliness.

On the twenty-fifth of Kislev, which is usually late in December, Jewish people celebrate the Festival of Light, Chanukah. This is a time of celebration—eight days of fun and feasting, and the exchange of gifts. During this time, Jewish homes glow with the light of Chanukah candles. An eight-branched candlestick—the Menorah—is used. On the first night, one candle is lighted from the shamash (the lighter) which is then set in its special place in the Menorah. On each succeeding night, one more candle is lighted, until all eight are aglow.

This candle-lighting ceremony goes back about 2000 years, when Antiochus Epiphanes, King of Syria, ruled all that remained of the Kingdom of Judah—and he demanded that all of his subjects worship the Greek gods. The Jews refused, and Judas Maccabeus led them in successful revolt. The Jews were again able to worship in the Temple of Jerusalem. The great Menorah was restored to its place. But when the Jews went to relight the Perpetual Light, they discovered that all but one cruse of holy oil had been defiled. There was only enough oil for one day, but when it was lighted, a miracle occurred: the oil burned for the full eight days needed to replenish the supply of holy oil. In commemoration, the eight-day festival was proclaimed. And it was called Chanukah, which means "dedication."

BIRTHDAYS. No birthday is complete without candles on the cake—and let no other candles interfere with this tradition. But there are special birthday candles which you may do for gifts or table decorations—and here are some ideas for them.

CANDLE CAKE. Make or buy a large round candle, about the size of a coffee can. Melt wax and color it pink or blue, then whip it into snow (See Chapter 1) and cover the "cake." When the wax snow is hard, stand birthday candles in holders in a circle around the top of the larger candle. These will burn down first—and can be blown out for good wishes. Then the larger candle will go on burning for hours. (See Illustration 9.)

BIRTHDAY-GO-ROUND. Make or buy a round candle about the size of a coffee can or cottage-cheese container. With sequins or bright beads make scallops around the top to give a canopy effect. As on a merry-go-round, of course! Run a band of sequins or beads about ½ inch above the base to indicate a floor line. Buy five metal horse-and-riders, or other figures if you prefer. Place them at intervals on the floor line. Now make five paper pennants, and letter them, as Happy Tenth Birthday to Jane, *one* word to a pennant. Attach the pennants to corsage pins with points fixed so that the metal figures appear to be carrying them. Angle the pins a little way out from the candle, and there you are.

GOOD WISHES CANDLE. Buy or make a round candle about the size of a coffee can or a square one of about the same size. Decorate the sides with a series of charms—such as you buy to put in cakes. A wishbone for good luck. A coin for wealth. A bluebird for happiness. And so on. (Don't arrange them in rows.) Between the charms, run festoons of sequins and stars, curving them gracefully, to make an overall pattern.

NAME CANDLES. Select a round squat candle about the size of a cottage-cheese container. Around top and bottom, run a row of silver stars, setting every other one a little lower, as in a rickrack design. Buy the silver letters which come in sheets, and spell out the birthday name around the center of the candle—Mary Jane Reed, for instance. Stick on the letters with a little melted wax.

ZODIAC CANDLES. Select round, square, or patio candles about the size of a pint milk carton. Make a stencil of the sign of the zodiac you need, and trace this onto gold or silver paper. Cut it out and fasten to the side of the candle, slightly above the center line. Frame it in braid or sequins. Use a square, round, or oval frame—whichever suits design and candle best. If you like, put a zodiac sign on each side of a square candle.

BIRTHDAY-CANDLE CANDLES. Select round or square candles about the size of a pint milk carton. Get small birthday candles of a contrasting shade. Fasten these with melted wax in close-rank formation around the base of the large candle. Above the wick of each little candle put a sequin or star in place of flame, for the birthday candles are not for lighting—just for good wishes. Scatter a few more sequins or stars above them on the sides of the large candle.

FLOWER TAPERS. Buy the long slim tapers which are meant to be used with flowers. Decorate them with glittering sequins, fastened on with melted wax since the candles are too slim to take pins. Present them with a bouquet of flowers, if you like.

BIRTHSTONE CANDLES. Candles which are 8 to 12 inches high do well here. Find dime-store rings with stones simulating the proper birthstone. You'll want three of these, and the stones should be large. Set these equidistant about 2 inches above the base of the candle (don't count the part which goes into the holder). With gold or silver sealing wax, fashion a setting for the stones. (See Chapter 2 for use of sealing wax on candles.)

BIRTHDAY FLOWER CANDLES. Buy artificial flowers —carnations for January, violets for February, daffodils for March, and so on. Wax them according to the directions in Chapter 2. Wire wreaths of flowers around the base of the candles, or make corsages to place near the base.

PAPER-DOLL CANDLES. For a little girl who is having a birthday. Cut a row of holding-hand paper dolls from gold or silver foil. Fasten them around a candle about the size of a coffee can. (They can be pinned on or sealed on with melted wax.) Give them hats of tiny waxed flowers or of sequins. Such decorations are for use on a well-burning candle, and very gay they are.

> *Year Counter: There's an old superstition which says that if you light a candle for the husband, and one the same size for the wife, the one which burns longest tells who will have the longer life.*

SHOWERS—WEDDINGS—ANNIVERSARIES. Many of the candles already described are attractive for these occasions, or for gift-giving at these times—flower candles, jeweled candles, monogrammed candles, to name some of them. Here are ideas to add to the list.

SHOWER CANDLES. Select a candle not less than 12 inches tall—and even taller is better. Buy the tiny paper umbrellas used for party favors—those which are open. Clip off the handles, and replace with corsage pins inserted through the umbrella tops. Cluster the umbrellas attractively near the candle base, fastening them in place with the pins. If the tapers are very tall, some umbrellas may be placed a little higher.

BRIDAL CANDLES. White, rough-textured candles, with a cluster of waxed, artificial orange blossoms at the base are simple and elegant. Spiral a few flowers a short way up the candle for a graceful look.

Or spiral lilies-of-the-valley about a third of the way up from the base of white rope candles. Use a few green leaves for contrast.

Or decorate creamy-white candles with pearl-bead

motifs. You can find ready-made medallions in dime stores, millinery shops, or at the trimming counters of department stores. Attach the medallions with melted wax, and set a few additional pearls in place with wax around the medallion to give a finishing touch.

> ☙ *Added Note: Emkay makes a Wedding Cake Candle in white and silver—designed to be burned on the wedding day, and relighted on each anniversary. Which is a nice idea, I think.*

PAPER TAPER. For the first anniversary. Cut three frills—like lamb chop frills—from a foreign-language paper, curling them gently with a table knife. Fasten them one above the other—leaving a little space between—at the base of the candle of your choice. Pin each frill in place with a pennant glued to a corsage pin, reading (*one* word to each pennant), Happy First Anniversary.

> ☙ *Paper Postscript: If the friends who are celebrating their first anniversary have a fireplace, why not also make them some old-fashioned paper spills for lighting the fire? For these, you need a long knitting needle and strips of newspaper cut about 1½ inches wide. Wind the paper tightly around the needle, overlapping it at each turn. Paste together any new strip which is added. Bend over the final end and secure it with a bit of glue. Pull out the needle, and you have an old-fashioned paper spill. You might make a paper cone from decorative paper for carrying purposes. Add a loop at the seam side of the cone so that it can be hung up.*

COTTON CANDLES. For the second anniversary. Buy half a dozen small vespers candles—more if you like! Melt wax and color it with white crayons. Whip it into snow (or in this case cotton), as directed in Chapter 1, and cover the small candles. Around the center of each run a gay band of cotton-ball fringe, fastened on with pins.

LEATHER LINES. For the third anniversary. Decorate heavy candles with bands of different colored leather fastened with melted wax, one above the other, from the base of the candle up. Or cut out leather designs and appliqué with hot wax to the candle sides. You can do the same kind of thing with patio candles.

FRUIT AND FLOWER CANDLES. For the fourth anniversary. You will find a number of floral decorations earlier in the book. Miniature fruits—from millinery counters or old hats—can be fastened into wreaths for the base of candles. Decor-Lite's Magic Circle candleholders make a good base for wiring the fruits in place. Later the decorations can be removed and the holders used as before.

SILK AND SILVER. Silk or silverware is appropriate for the fifth anniversary. You can do amusing decorations around a large square candle with the tiny doll silverware sold in toy shops and dime stores. Run a band of silver braid about an inch above the base of the candle. Just above this—but not touching—on each side, do a place setting, fastening knife, fork, and spoon in place with melted wax, or decorate with a doll's tea service. Run a second band of silver braid above the settings.

If you prefer silk, fashion wire mesh into a globe about

the size of an orange. Leave a center hole so as to fit globe over a candleholder, and through which the candle will go. Cover the wire with a froufrou of silk ruffling, sewn on. When finished, a ball of ruffles adorns the candle base. Use a tall candle.

WOOD WORKERS. For the sixth anniversary. In hardware or upholstery shops, buy wooden-headed upholstery pins to stud the sides of heavy candles. . . . Wax on tiny wooden rolling pins or miniature clothespins. . . . Or fasten on wooden beads with pins which have large, decorative heads. . . . Small pieces of driftwood can be used for the central motif of a design at the base of a heavy square candle, with shells and pebbles to complete it.

> *Did you know that finely split, pitch-filled wood, used in a fireplace, is called candlewood? In the old days, a good deal of homework was done by the flaring light of the candlewood, tossed a few splinters at a time on top of the blazing logs. And thrifty homemakers saved many a precious candle in this way.*

COPPER CANDLES. For the seventh anniversary. Copper wire lends itself admirably to candle decorating. And so does the thin sheet copper which can be cut with scissors into flat patterns for appliquéing to the sides of candles with melted wax. Copper wire can be wrapped in ringlike bands at intervals around the lower part of candles, or bent into amusing pictures (rather like line drawings) and then pinned to the candle with short pieces of wire doubled, brad-fashion, over the wire of the picture, the free ends stuck into the candle.

CANDLE BRONZE. For the eighth anniversary. You can use bronze-headed upholstery nails here. Some of them are very handsome indeed and easy to work into interesting patterns for the heavier candles. For tapers, clip off the nail part and apply the heads with melted wax. (Nails are thick and apt to damage slender candles.) Run a vertical line of three or four nailheads up the side of a candle from just above the base. Or set three rings of heads, slightly separated, near the base of the candle. Or decorate candles with bronze sealing wax. (See method in Chapter 2.) You can also use bronze coins or bronze miniatures attached with melted wax.

NOTES FOR NINE. The ninth anniversary is either leather (see our third anniversary notes), or pottery. You can get a ceramic effect with sealing-wax flowers or figures, made as described in Chapter 2. Or you can use a piece of ceramic jewelry as the central motif in a design. In this case, you are giving an extra gift.

TIN IS FOR TEN. Thin sheets of tin or shiny tin cans can be cut with tin-cutting shears into various patterns. For a large, square or round well-burning candle, cut a scalloped edging to go around the candle about half an inch up from the base. Bend it at the corners for a square candle so that it will fit, and fasten it by punching holes in the tin and pinning on the decoration or just fasten on with melted wax. Above this border, apply cutouts of geometric shape, monograms, medallions, stylized flowers, or even tin doll dishes.

CRYSTAL CANDLES. Plastic prisms make lovely fifteenth-anniversary candles. Select tall tapers. A spiral mobile of wire gives one pleasant effect. (See page 69.) Fasten the prisms with fine silver cord—just a tiny loop of it—glued to the wire where you want the prism to dangle. Carry the wire spiral only two-thirds of the way up the candle, for when the candle burns down to the top of the wire, it is finished until the decoration is removed.

Or multiply the candle flame with prisms on a wire frame rather like an *inverted* lamp shade. Select 12-inch candles. Make a wire cone about 1½ inches shorter than the candle (don't count the section that goes into the holder). Make the wider circle of the cone about 6 inches across. Make the circle for the smallest part of the inverted cone just large enough to fit around the candle above the base. Fasten the two circles together with four straight pieces of wire long enough to make a cone of proper height. Set them equidistant. Then, for firmness, fasten guy wires half-way down on the cone. Cover all wires—except the guy wires—with glue and sprinkle with silver glitter. Let dry. Wire prisms around the top circle, working carefully. Now place the candle in the inverted cone, drawing it up through the small, lower circle.

Complete the fastening of the guy wires just the way you would if you were using them to hold a Christmas tree straight: Hold the cone straight, run the guy wire around the candle, fasten to the vertical wire directly opposite. Repeat with the other guy wire. Clip off excess wire. Spread the guy wire with glue. Cover with glitter. Let dry. Then fasten additional prisms to these guy wires.

One last thing: Do a bit of finishing by touching up each wire holding a prism with a little glue, a little glitter. And if, in fastening the guy wires, any glitter has chipped off, patch these places, too. This decoration is not difficult.

Just be sure, when tightening guy lines, that the cone stands straight.

SILVER LIGHT. For the twenty-fifth anniversary. Run bands of silver braid around a tall candle. On a short, heavy, well-burning candle, place vertical bands; or apply the braid in an allover geometric design. . . . Or pin or wax on silver cord in an embroidery pattern. Medallions and filigree patterns can be clipped from silver lace-paper doilies and waxed into place, or glued to patio candles.

There is another fairy-like trick to do with the lace-paper-doily decorations: First spray the doily with plastic or shellac it. When it is dry, clip out snowflake patterns—none of them much bigger than a quarter, some of them smaller. Use a rope candle, and pin these like dangles along the twisted ridges—the highest one not over half-way up the candle.

Candles for the twenty-fifth anniversary can be coated with silver glitter. (Paint on melted wax, or dip and drain, then sprinkle the glitter while the wax is still warm enough to hold it.) Silver flowers can cluster at candle bases, or climb part way up a tall candle. . . . Silver coins can be waxed to the sides of well-burning candles. You might use the inexpensive silver coins found on dime-store charm bracelets. Or you might set ten dimes in a ring around a large candle.

There are paper brads which have a silvery look and can be used for studding (so can thumbtacks). . . . And silver metal costume jewelry from the dime store can always be commanded for your use. They're very satisfactory candles to do—these silvery ones. And the silver sparkles in the candle flame. The basic color of your candle can be whatever you desire—or whatever will match the party decorative scheme. And P.S.—You will use these candles for other occasions, too.

GOLDEN GLEAM. For a fiftieth anniversary. Select a square, creamy-white, well-burning candle. Clip gold medallions from a gold, lace-paper doily. Set these over the sides of the candle, with a small, gold, Christmas-tree ball pinned to the center of each; a row of gold beading, top and bottom, to finish.

Or gild miniature fruits and fashion them into wreaths to go around the bases of tall white tapers. . . . On a well-burning candle, set, with melted wax, gilt charms which symbolize happy events of the fifty years. Frame each charm with gold cord or braid. Take time in selecting the events. Try to get dates for each, and underneath each framed charm, print the date in gilt paint. You will have provided a wealth of memories, stimulation for nostalgic conversation, and also a lovely candle gift.

DIAMOND BRIGHT. For the diamond jubilee. Stud a white taper with sparkling rhinestones, pinned on or waxed in place. . . . Cluster them thickly at the base with only a few scattered above like winking stars. . . . Set the two names and the date of the marriage in rhinestones on a white pillar candle. . . . Buy a globe candle (snowball). Gild it. Deck it with rhinestones. . . . Glue rhinestones to a wire and curl it two-thirds of the way up a slim white taper. . . . Glue rhinestones to the outside of a patio candle, so that they shine and glitter as the light burns down.

In this flame, all memory;
Candle burn in jubilee;
And in content—
Love-sent. . . .

OTHER SPECIAL DAYS. There are candles for other special days, too, and let's go around the calendar with them. How shall we say it? I light one candle for laughter, and one for tears; one for reverence, and one for remembering. I light a candle for sorrow, and for celebration—and on holidays I light a handful of them just to be glad!

NEW YEAR, which is the beginning. We don't often give New Year's presents, but we always give New Year's greetings, and why aren't candles happy messengers? A traditional candle, perhaps, which will be brought out year after year, and another section burned each year in remembrance of good friends and old times with the hope of happy tomorrows together.

Select a tall, heavy pillar candle—one of those which is slightly smaller at the top than at the base. Mark off at about 1½-inch intervals. (This is not an exact figure; it depends on the candle height; sections must come out even.) Pin (with lengths of wire doubled to form brads) a ring of silver bells along each section line. In silver paint print the years ahead, first the year just beginning in the top section which will burn down first. Paint on as many years as the candle affords. Each year only the proper part will be burned. Then the candle will be put away to wait for another year to start. When friends gather together on New Year's Eve, the special candle can be lit at midnight as they begin to sing the familiar, always-new words of *Auld Lang Syne.*

Here is another traditional candle for New Year's giving. It takes a bit of doing, but you may like it. This candle must be made—so see Chapter 1 for directions. Mold it in round sections about 1½ inches deep. Have as many sections as you like—and as the candle proportions will bear. Then from thin sheets of copper cut circles of the same size as the candle, and as many as you have candle segments. Pierce ½-inch holes in the center of each disk, rather like a Chinese coin. On each disk write, in enamel, a New Year's wish for the coming year. Put candles and disks together, fastening them with melted wax. The last disk goes at the base of the candle. Place the disks message-side down.

Insert the candle wick—and this is the reason for the center hole in the sheet-copper disks. When the candle is completed, decorate it by running a band of good wishes around each line of juncture. You make the bands by cutting ½-inch strips of sheet copper. Write on them good-wish jingles of your own. Then wax the bands in place.

When the candle has burned to the first disk, it is, of course, the New Year's start. The flame is blown out. The copper disk is removed, and the wish for the year ahead read. It's rather fun—simple, homely fun, and I don't know a better kind. And it's good each year to find a new message from an old friend in a candle which burns steadily. Just one thing: Do handle this candle carefully. It's rather fragile.

Did you know that Candlemas Day—February 2—began way back in the eleventh century? On this day, candles are blessed, and Scripture read describing the candle as a symbol of love for the indwelling Christ.

VALENTINE CANDLES. And may they be romantic! You can, as noted in Chapter 1, make your own heart-shaped candles. You can buy them, too—perhaps through a special order given ahead unless your candle shop carries a good stock. Here are ideas to dress up valentine candles: Cut wax medallions, heart-shaped, and fasten them to the sides of pillar candles with melted wax. (See Chapter 2). . . . Or make gold and silver heart mobiles for

tall tapers. Let some of them be just silhouettes of hearts. . . . Make your own valentine on the side of a patio candle. There are valentine kits, or if you scorn them, glue on your own design—paper lace, cupids, hearts, mottoes, and all. Glue them right on the glass of the patio candle. And you can do a similar kind of designing on large, square or round well-burning candles.

Make a sequin heart on the side of a large, square candle, outlining it in sequins. Letter your message in tiny beads. Pierce the heart with an arrow made from a corsage pin with a bit of feather glued to the head, and a gilt paper tip at the end. (The tip will actually be about ¾ inch above the point of the pin. You stick that part of the pin into the candle to hold the arrow in place.)

Do a dressmaker-dummy candle (and apologies to Schiaparelli!). Select about a 12-inch candle 2½ inches in diameter. Beat up some wax snow (see Chapter 1)—shocking pink, maybe? Mold it, dressmaker-dummy style, circa 1890—they were gay. When the wax snow has hardened, embellish your creation with a jeweled necklace, a few sparkling sequins, and a heart of gold, appropriately placed and lettered. It can be stabbed in place with a jeweled hat pin. And very good fun this candle is, too.

You can do either romantic or amusing valentine candles by drawing on the large ones with sealing wax. (See Chapter 2.) Or you can draw with crayons dipped in flame to the melting point. (Better practice first.) The sealing wax will give a more embossed look—and the drawing can be finer.

Remember the little candy-heart mottoes—which are harder to get now than they used to be? They make gay, if rather unorthodox, candle decorations. Just decide on a pattern and wax them in place. You might wax a red cord casually around them to make a frame. Short, heavy well-burning candles are best for this kind of decoration. You can use tapers if you keep decorations low. The mottoes on those candy hearts always did make entertaining reading, and so they do as candle decoration.

EASTER. And, of course, Easter-egg candles. Basic directions for making them are given in Chapter 1. You can buy ready-made Easter-egg candles, too. Decorating either is fun. Do them up with sequins. Pin on braid. Paint them with sealing wax or melted crayons. Set a ring of tiny flowers around the base, and a few sequins up above. Fasten on colored paper dots with melted wax. Dip the candles so there are two colors, and run a dividing line of cord around the middle. In short, just go ahead and have fun. These little candles make good party favors, by the way. One at each place setting.

Candles for the Easter dinner table should, I think, be simply decorated. White waxed flowers and green leaves done in wreath- or corsage-fashion are good. (See Chapter 2.) Spring-flower decorations are always lovely—use artificial, waxed flowers. Simple designs in gold have an elegant look. You might cover the glass of patio candles with an allover pattern of gold lace, clipped from paper doilies. Here and there, but sparingly, add a few tiny flowers. . . . Gold crosses may be cut from metallic paper and glued to patio candles or waxed to other candles. Frames of braid or cord may be used around them.

In the Catholic Church, at the first Mass of the Resurrection on Holy Saturday, the impressive Paschal Candle is lighted. This large and beautiful candle represents Christ, the true light. The

smaller candles used are typical of each individual who strives to reproduce Christ in his life. The Paschal Candle is burned until Ascension Day, when it is extinguished.

For informal occasions, try your hand at molding a wax lamb. You will need a mold such as is used for Easter dessert. (In Chapter 1 are wax formulas and basic instructions.) . . . You can make quite a bunny from two globe (snowball) candles. The small one makes the head; the larger, about 2½ inches in diameter, makes the body. Figure out just where you want to place the head candle. With a knife, flatten the larger candle at this point. Similarly, flatten one side of the smaller candle. Stick the two together with melted wax. (To reinforce this joining, run part of a cocktail pick into the large globe, then into the head ball—with, of course the hot wax used for gluing in place.)

Now fashion two ears from white paper, and attach them with pins to the head. Place them rakishly. Part of a bunny's engaging character is in the set of his ears. Clip off the wick from the smaller candle. Draw on a bunny face with melted crayons. Make whiskers from fine wire, brush with glue, and sprinkle with glitter—varicolored glitter, maybe, just for the sake of being unexpected. Add a blob of waxed snow for a tail. It's the larger candle which is lighted.

JULY FOURTH. Of course, make a firecracker candle. Select a plain red, round candle—of firecracker proportions. (It can be a large firecracker.) And that's all. But when the season is right, and your table settings appropriate, it *is* a firecracker.

Patio candles are usually good for July-fourth candles, for this is outdoor-eating time. Decorating the glass is easy. Apply decals of flags, bunting, firecrackers, or whatever is available—and suitable. Or paint on your July-fourth scenes with enamel or glass paint. You can suggest some pretty lively fireworks with a little freehand drawing, and a few sequins glued on. . . . If you like, you could paint the opening bars of *The Star-Spangled Banner*—words and music—on a patio candle.

For a gala July-fourth outdoor party, do a sparkler candle. Get a squat, square, heavy red candle. Buy long sparklers—the kind you had when you were young. Paint the wire stems red. Stick them, like porcupine quills, around the base of the candle (not so close to the bottom that they will break the wax). Pin a few silver stars to the outside of the candle. When party time comes, light the candle—and light the sparklers, too. (You know they "spark," but the sparks don't burn.) Don't light all the sparklers at once and as each burns out withdraw it—until all are used. Sort of fun, eating by sparkler light. Need I add that such candles require plenty of space?

HALLOWEEN. There are special commercial candles for this day, so check with your local shop, but you might want to make your own jack-o'-lantern candles. Use vertically fluted gelatin molds. (See Chapter 1 for Basic Formulas, and for use of molds.) Tint the wax orange color. Make two molds and seal them together, matching the fluting as you do. Paint faces on the jack-o'-lanterns with black crayon, melted at the point and then used with quick, sure strokes. These little candles are fun for individual place candles at a table. Set them on dark-green coasters or saucers which will look attractive—and catch any dripping from the wax.

Try your hand at making a ghost candle. Mold the candle in a metal tumbler. (See Chapter 1 for Basic Formulas.) Color the wax with white crayons. When it is set, but not hard, dip the glass in very hot water and slide the wax out. Now working quickly before the wax sets, model the general form of a ghost. Moot point: what shape is a ghost? I have in mind the sheeted variety with hooded head. Mold the wax on the body to indicate draping. Pinch in the wax to form the neck. With an orangewood stick press in the outline of the hood and give your ghost a little round face, framed by the hood. Let the candle harden completely, then insert the prepared wick, from the top of the head down. Paint in the face with black crayon.

Old Superstition: When the candle burns blue, ghosts walk. So beware!

THANKSGIVING. Gilded grains make attractive decorations (sometimes you can buy artificial ones), or you might use headed grasses. Or both. For example: Select ripe heads of wheat—and this is a matter of advance planning. Dry, dip in wax, and gild when the wax has hardened. Also select a number of stiff, spiky grasses and gild them. Using melted wax, set them around the base of a pillar candle—a head of grain, a spike or two of grass, and so on, working them into an attractive pattern. You can also fashion grain and grass from sealing wax as described in Chapter 2.

Artificial grapes and leaves can be used on Thanksgiving candles. Twine them around a fairly tall candle—near the base—wiring them in place. Or make wreaths of them to go around the bases of your candles. You might glue a bunch of grapes and two or three leaves to the side of patio candles.

Try molding a turkey candle. (See Chapter 1 for Basic Formulas.) Begin with a globe not more than $2\frac{1}{2}$ inches in diameter. Let it harden. Melt extra wax and let it set, but not harden. It should be about $\frac{1}{2}$ inch thick. Cut two circles, place one on top of the other, and set the globe on them, pressing it into the wax slightly so that the circles of wax act as a base. Cut another circle from the set-but-not-hard wax, large enough to make a fanned-out tail for the turkey. (Size depends on the size of the globe.) Mold this to the globe candle—in the appropriate position! Use extra melted wax as needed, and mold the tail with your fingers to get a realistic look. Cut another piece from the sheet of wax for the head, and mold it into place. If the sheet gets too hard to handle, set it over hot water. Finally draw on wing lines with an orangewood stick. When you have finished, insert a wick down the center of the globe candle. With a brush, paint the turkey with melted crayons.

And did you know that in Bulgaria it is the custom on Christmas Eve for each peasant to take a lighted candle to the barn to waken the animals with the greeting: "The Child is born, and blesses you tonight"?

How inferior for *seeing* with,
is your brightest train of fireworks
to the humblest farthing candle!

THOMAS CARLYLE

IV

Candles and Flowers

HOW TO DECORATE WITH CANDLES IN YOUR HOME

THE BRIDE on whom the sun shines may be the happy bride—though I am unwilling to go along with the idea that her happiness depends on the weather. But certainly the home with candlelight is a gracious home, and the candlelit occasion, a pleasant one.

We have made our candles now—and we have decorated those which we have either made or purchased. Now comes the wonderful business of decorating *with* them—for candles are to be used, not just seen. So we place them in our homes with a thought to graciousness, a thought to good fellowship, a thought for the lovely charm which is everlasting.

No one book—and certainly not this one—pretends to give all the good decorating ideas which there may be. They are as various as the homes in which they appear, and as individual as the women who arrange them. You will have many ideas which I will not think of. I may have some which you may wish to borrow. Together we will light the candles of remembrance and of future hopes, of simplicity and of elegance. And I think this is a pleasant kind of thing to share. I hope that you will, too.

FLOWERS AND CANDLES. Let's begin with some charming decorations from Margaret Carrick of Los Angeles. Hers is a fresh approach—a wellspring of inspiration for all who enjoy working with flowers. Perhaps you know her treasure of a book, *Creative Flower Arranging,* published by M. Barrows and Company, Inc.

Kitchen Garden Luncheon: Imagination, for instance, is displayed in her kitchen-garden luncheon table. (Illustration 16.) You've noticed—haven't we all?—the red, red roses climbing over the wall for a peek at the kitchen garden. Mrs. Carrick capitalizes artistically on this. She selects a handcrafted Mexican cloth in beige and white. (If you cannot get one quite so elegant, you may find an interesting copy which will be pleasantly inexpensive.) She selects plates and candleholder in pale-yellow and warm-oatmeal, and she does her centerpiece to accent these homely colors.

As a base for her arrangement, she chooses a chopping block of sanded white hardwood, banded with a thin strip of stainless steel—and don't worry if your block isn't brand-new. It's the color and texture of the scrubbed wood which gives the pleasant quality. For the candles, Mrs. Carrick uses an interesting four-pronged holder, simple in design but not too ordinary. The candles are in four colors, all geared to her wood-and-ivory theme.

On the chopping block, she arranges her kitchen-garden

decor: a cucumber, a shiny green pepper, an elegant red onion, a snowy-white cauliflower—all of which go well with the color of natural wood. Then she adds the note which lifts the whole thing from the ordinary and makes it a conversation piece. Pinned to the cauliflower is a single, rich-red rose, full-blown as a Spanish senorita. And as gay. A simple touch? Yes, if imagination is simple. But one of those things we remember.

And a postscript to this: Suppose you'd like to add a few flowers from your garden to such an arrangement; just punch a hole in the bell pepper, fill it with water, stick in the posies. And there you are! No manmade container necessary. And rather fun whether you copy this setting or do one of your own.

Spring party: Mrs. Carrick gives us a charming spring setting with both simplicity and grace. (Illustration 17.) Tall creamy candles—the beeswax ones which seem to hold light within themselves—are set in stark-white pottery candlesticks. Note that the candleholders are not the same height. One is taller than the other, and this is a good basic decorative idea. It's often wise to avoid the symmetrical, the even, the "sets."

Flanking the candles, and set on a cloth which features vegetable forms in chalk-white against a dull, gray-blue background, is a flower arrangement of yellow iris, golden daffodils, variegated privet, and apricot-colored ranunculus. To this, Mrs. Carrick adds dusty miller foliage and buds.

The container is of dark, smoky-green-blue glass—which ties all the colors rather handsomely together. For one added touch, she introduces a fat little teapot in white with a bamboo handle.

Camellia Pyramid: Or try Mrs. Carrick's tiered arrangement of pink camellias, saxifrage, apple-blossom viburnum, and tiny sprigs of wax flowers. She arranges them in two stacked compotes with a small container at the top to hold the "upright" flowers. From the top, too, a tall pink candle which sheds a soft warm glow over a tea table. The compotes are muted blue-purple with flecks of gold, and lovely with the soft-pink flowers. A Japanese tea set of deep-blue lined with white completes a simple but effective picture. And do note how some of the flowers rise high against the candle, so there is no abrupt ending, no sense of sudden change.

Bird-Cage Candle: Mrs. Carrick uses black wire accessories now so easily found in the shops for another intriguing arrangement of candles and flowers. (Illustration 20.) She selects a simple container with a curved-cone, black-wire base, the bowl itself edged with lacy loops of wire. Next to it, and hung from the ceiling, is a black-wire candle ball—a bird-cage candleholder, as it is sometimes called, and quite literally a black-wire adaptation of a Japanese lantern. (If you've not yet met these, do get acquainted with them.) The arrangement is one which you can make up with your own garden flowers —big, big dahlias of deep, glowing pink and dark, dark red. A few bold, strong leaves from dark-red cannas, and a filigree of grayed-lavender caspia by way of contrast. There's a fat, pink candle in the black-wire globe—and the whole arrangement is one you can do in minutes, and for which you will gather praise for hours.

Magic Moment: Let's do one more Margaret Carrick flower-and-candle arrangement, another conversation piece. (Color Plate II.) Begin with a white compote—clean in line, simple in design. In this stand a pinholder, and in it a tall creamy candle, delicately modeled. Heat the pinholder before placing the candle on it. Around the base of the candle arrange three plump white-tissue balls (the kind which fold flat, and open up engagingly). These have been fastened to the pinholder. In the low, flat bowl of the compote, also arrange Christmas-tree balls—some rather large, some in small clusters like grapes. Stand a spray of lacy gray caspia in the holder, its delicate tracery reaching up along the candle's length. Then, to complete this design, attach to the candle, by curved wires, colorful foil moths, which seem to hover close but never actually touch the lovely and delicate design.

Pink Heather: If you would like to try a lovely and easily copied arrangement, try one which Colonial Candles has done for us. (Illustration 13.) Select a low round bowl, and in it arrange a charming assortment of heather and pink carnations, with interesting, broad-leafed foliage to tie all together. The heather rises high in the background. The carnations cluster close at the front of the design. A varicolored selection of Colonial flower tapers, from deep mauve to palest pink, fan out through the bouquet, which is placed in a slightly arched holder. This arrangement is simple to do—and most effective.

Flower-Bower: And you might turn a low, graceful candelabrum into an interesting flower-bower. Take a block of Non-spillable Water (a commercial product whose trade name is Oasis—ask your florist), and wrap the base of it in a double layer of foil, with a piece of newspaper in between. This is to absorb excess moisture.

Set the block in the central, low-curved part of the candelabrum. (If there is a center candle, cut the block to go around it.) Next make your arrangement, sticking the flowers into the block (which will keep them fresh).

You might begin with four or five graceful stalks of stock, setting them low and in an outward spray so they form something of a circle. Fill in with short-stemmed carnations, shaping your arrangement so that it covers the block and complements the candelabrum. Add a few strands of graceful vine to complete the picture. Tapers, of course, in the candelabrum. And you do not have to choose the flowers here suggested. Work with any you like, needless to say. The Non-spillable Water gives you a chance to do any number of interesting displays. It can be cut to shape, and flowers can be arranged in it without any trouble.

Autumn Supper: Let's look at an attractive arrangement Will & Baumer does, using three long-burning Taperlite candles in an antique candelabrum to dominate a supper setting. Tall tapers rise behind a centerpiece, lovely in gently-shaded colors: deep-pink carnations, mauve asters, copper-colored chrysanthemums, cycad, and green grapes arranged in a Victorian silver cake basket. (If you have been wondering what to do with the one great-grandmother left, here is one answer.)

Don't be tempted to substitute colored candles—for the pure-white ones lend a touch of elegance it would be rather a pity to miss. Bone china has been used on the table, amethyst glassware to complement the asters, and a dark-green skirted tablecloth to give a perfect background. This is the kind of setting which anyone may copy, and with most satisfying results. (See Illustration 22.)

Snack Buffet: Will & Baumer also does a snack buffet with Twistolite candles in turquoise pottery holders on a serve-yourself sideboard. It features a fall arrangement of gay chrysanthemums in an Italian ceramic bowl, with heavy

Plate I. Jeweled patio candle by Avis Stendal; flower-studded sealing wax candle, and tall sealing-wax-decorated taper by Alice Jaffe; sequin-trimmed taper, shell-decorated pillar candle, and star-decked cone by Frederick-Thomas; homemade lavender candle and ice-blue driftwood candle by Michael Powers; at the right, another of Mrs. Jaffe's tapers.

Plate II. Foil moths flutter around a tall creamy taper; tissue balls, frosted Christmas-tree decorations and a lacy spray of gray caspia to complete the picture. (Setting by Margaret Carrick, California.)

Plate III. A red candle set in a Styrofoam ball tops the Italian glass bottle; a snowball candle stands at the base. Mexican straw beads spiral from one to the other. (Setting by Margaret Carrick, California.)

foliage added for necessary height, a cluster of grapes dripping from one side and down over two golden-yellow gourds. A pale-yellow cloth gives a wonderful background, and brown earthenware adds just the right color touch to complete the picture. You will notice that candles and flowers have been placed to enhance, but not to interfere with the serving. And this, obvious though it may seem, is something hostesses too often forget. (See Illustration 23.)

"Cardinal's Hat": Here is a fall-flower-and-grape-cluster setting for dinner by candlelight, also by Will & Baumer. (See Illustration 24.) The centerpiece is arranged on a pewter "cardinal's hat"—one actually used by Ethan Allen. But you may use whatever round tray you have—in bronze, for instance, or copper. Stand a low container on it—off center. Cluster fat bunches of grapes around it. Then place your chrysanthemums in a rather low arrangement, with some flowers hugging the grapes. Use sprigs of foliage for height.

On each side of the centerpiece stand Twistolite candles—these are set in a pair of Bristol lusters, which are truly handsome. The shining crystal prisms catch and hold the lovely candlelight. Green and white china is set on simple place mats. And in the background, standing on the polished sideboard, antique girandoles hold dark-green Taperlite candles. There you have it—a setting for a family dinner with company manners—or a company dinner with family charm.

Gleam of Copper: Some Saturday night when you are having a lentil-soup-hot-French-bread-with-garlic-butter-fruit-cheese-and-coffee supper, let your table decor suit the mood. Fill two copper ring molds with the dessert fruit—pears, apples, grapes. Set one ring at each end of the table, and in the center of each, stand a pillar candle, perhaps in sunny yellow, perhaps in deep-green.

Sea Scenes: When you are having a clam-chowder-and-roast-corn dinner, let your centerpiece remind you of the beach. Set a rectangular mirror in the center of the table. In one corner, arrange three large clam shells so that they overlap and look attractive. Glue them securely in place. In each, set a white rope candle, and let them be of different heights, with the tallest not more than 6 or 7 inches. Secure them to the shells with melted wax. In the opposite corner of the mirror, (without the shell holders) set two more rope candles, slightly shorter than those you have already placed. On the mirror itself, complete the design with a scattering of small shells, colored pebbles, a starfish if you have one. Very easy to do and rather fun.

Fountain Centerpiece: For spring, place a round mirror in the center of your table. Cut two round pieces of Non-spillable Water, one slightly larger than the other (size will depend on size of mirror, but 3 and 4 inches will be about right). Fasten the smaller to the larger by driving a couple of wooden skewers through both. Cover bottom and sides of the larger circle with that crinkly paper florists put around flower pots—and you've now made the base of the fountain. It goes in the center of the mirror. In it, arrange white lilacs or lilies-of-the-valley to give an effect of fountain spray. Around the mirror set floating candles of your choice.

Arrange-O-Disc Delight: For candle-and-flower arrangements you might also get acquainted with the Candle Vase and Arrange-O-Disc. The clever little vase slips down over a candle and rests on the candlestick. With it comes a perforated disk—it looks much like the dial on a telephone—which can be fitted over the top of the vase to hold the flowers in place. Margaret Lo Piccolo, who owns The Candle Light, a wonderful candle shop in Fair Haven, New Jersey (and more about her later), recommends the Candle Vase and Arrange-O-Disc. Her slogan, by the way, is: "The charm of candlelight is like the fragrance of flowers" —which is, I should say, one reason why the two go so well together.

Mantel Design: Will & Baumer does a tall, formal arrangement of fall flowers, gourds, and foliage, with golden-yellow Twistolite candles, sun-bright highlights of the tall bouquet. (Illustration 27.) Note that one of the three candleholders is shorter than the other two, which is a good point to add to your decorating memos.

Sculptured Prism: Another good point, I think, is to get acquainted with the engaging Prisms made by the Victrylite Candle Company. These candles slowly transform themselves into sculptured beauty as they burn. The sides of the candles fold back into intriguing designs. (If you wish, you can mold the wax flow with your fingers to get any desired effect.) Interesting when used alone. Intriguing when used with feathery floral or foliage arrangements. (See Illustration 34.)

Candle Planter Bowl: A copper-and-brass specialty of The Candle Light shop, does marvelously well on mantel or table, and gives you a permanent, always-green setting for a pillar candle. Plant with whatever foliage you like, and change the color of your candle from time to time by way of variety. (See Illustration 14.)

Americana: If your home boasts Early American furniture, look at Illustration 26 for a setting which fits perfectly with the theme. Here you have Will & Baumer's bayberry candle throwing off the sweet scent of the wax berries from which it was made, recreating the soft light in which our forefathers lived and worked. The adjustable iron candlestick is flanked by a pistol tinder lighter and a wooden candlebox, containing cotoneaster. The pine chest was once a Quaker washstand. And the simplicity of the setting is a great part of its charm. No frills nor furbelows; no non-essentials to distract the eye.

Did you know that a curious medieval practice of the Catholic Church was that of offering at a favored shrine a candle—or a number of candles—equaling in measurement the height of a person for whom some favor was asked? This was called "measuring to" such and such a saint (and may well be where our expression "measuring up" had its origin). The practice traces back to the time of St. Radegund in the sixth century, and was particularly common in England and the North of France in the twelfth and thirteenth centuries.

CHRISTMAS MANTELS. They are many and varied, and surely no home is complete without its candle decorations at Christmas time. Some are gay, some have simple beauty, some express the deep religious meaning of the day. Select your favorites, and light your candles as the old, familiar words remind us: "One for adoration; two for celebration."

Madonna Setting: This is one of Margaret Carrick's original settings. The base of the arrangement is a Lazy-Susan of blond wood. On this, she places a yellow mat of simple design. Slightly off center, she sets a low bowl holding branches of Chinese holly berries and glossy leaves. She uses an extra-large, green-yellow candle and pushes it down on the pins of a pinholder. (Mrs. Carrick recommends heating the pinholder and placing the candle first, to avoid possible splitting of the candle base.) In front of the candle and the arrangement, she stands a lovely Italian interpretation of a head of a Virgin, on an upturned ceramic container which acts as a pedestal.

Noel Blocks: Victrylite Paragon Noel Block candles are the inspiration for a Christmas mantel setting. These 3½-inch blocks spell out the word Noel—one letter to each block. They're fun to use just as they are, of course, but try giving them a gala setting some time. For instance: Make a set of steps from heavy cardboard, the top of each step about 4½ inches square, each riser about ¾ inch. Cover with gold paper. Stud the front side of the steps and the end with Christmas-tree balls. (Fasten the balls in place with paper brads. Put the wire loop of the ball through the brad, then the brad through the cardboard, opening it out on the inside of the steps. A sharp-pointed knife will expedite this last.) Place the steps on the left end of the mantel. Set a Noel Block on each step. Around the base, swirl a couple of strings of colored tree balls, letting one string extend out toward the center of the mantel. On the other end, place a gilded bowl of tree balls of various colors and sizes.

Candle Trains: Some Christmas card firms now offer gay little cardboard trains to hold the season's greeting cards. You can turn last year's into a candle train for the mantel with very little trouble. Cut one side from the engine and one from each of the cars. Pin the cutouts to the sides of heavy square candles. Stand them on the mantel, engine first—and not in too straight a line. Let them zigzag a bit. Couple the cars with short strings of tiny Christmas-tree balls. If you like, create two Christmas scenes with houses, a church, a barn, fences from a miniature village, the kind often used under the tree. Place the scenes at each end of the mantel, as if the train had just left one village and were approaching another.

Simple Beauty: At one end of the mantel, place five tapers in star-shaped glass holders, each candle a little shorter than the next—the tallest on the outside. At the other end, place a single taper, as high as the tallest one in your first group. Candles may be of the same shade or in gradations of color—whichever you like. And nothing more is needed for this quietly lovely arrangement.

Stars and Clouds: You will want nine candles—one very tall taper, and then pairs of successive heights down to about 6 inches. That wonderful clear ice-blue for the color, please. Decorate the candles with silver sequin stars, some larger, some smaller—and placed haphazardly, not in a formal pattern. Stand the candles in low, flat glass holders, and arrange them on the mantel—the tallest in the center, matching heights on each side down to the very shortest ones. At the base of the candles drift spun glass so that the candles seem to be rising from the clouds. (Spun glass, also called Angel's Hair, can be found in dime stores and decorating shops.) Sprinkle the spun glass with tiny silver star sequins which will dance and glimmer in the candlelight.

Holly-Ball Holders: Use these gay candleholders on mantel, hall table, corner whatnot, or sideboard. Or stand a couple of them on the dressing table of the guest room. With wire mesh, fashion four balls molded over low candleholders. Place a red candle in each holder, poking it through the mesh. Then cover each ball with holly leaves and clusters of bright red berries, wiring them in place. Be sure to place the candle before decorating, even though it seems a slightly backward procedure, for the candle helps hold the wire ball in shape. Stand the holly balls at intervals along the mantel. Or cluster three at one end (candles of different heights in this case), and one at the other end. Or pair them off, two by two. Use more holly on the mantel, if you like, and if the holly lacks colorful berries, wire on some artificial ones.

Reflections: This decoration is only for those who have mirrors hung over their mantels. You will need, to begin with, wooden skewers which you brush with glue and sprinkle with glitter; lengths of tinsel; and large Christmas-tree balls. The number of each will depend on the size of your mirror. Tape the glitter-covered skewers at intervals of about 4 inches along the top of the mirror so that they stick out at right angles. Or approximately that. If the mirror frame is not flat on top, the skewers will angle a little up or down, but this doesn't matter. And Mystik Tape, by the way, is a good fastener to use.

Now to each skewer, tie a length of tinsel. No two which are adjacent should be the same length—but the whole pattern should have balance so, for example, the end pieces of tinsel will be about the same length. At the end of each piece of tinsel tie a large Christmas-tree ball—and you may decorate these by gluing on sequins if you like. Or you might select some of those wonderfully elaborate Christmas balls which are on the market. On the mantel stand a line of candles in low holders, and let their heights vary too. Candle flames and Christmas balls multiply in the mirror, and the balls have an engaging tendency to turn endlessly in the heat of the candle flames as they are lit. By the way, do not have the glass balls too close to the flames for they may break.

Silver Tree and Vigil Light: Decorate a 12- to 14-inch artificial silver tree with a wealth of tiny Christmas-tree balls—as many as you can wire in place. Stand the tree in the center of the mantel. Arrange vigil lights at 4-inch intervals on each side of the tree. Decorate each by gluing tiny Christmas-tree balls to the glass containers—not too many here.

> *Did you know that it was an old Irish custom for the Christmas Eve candles to be lighted by the youngest child—or the one named Mary? Then the front door was left ajar for the Stranger who was expected, and welcomed by the living light.*

Sequin Snowstorm: For a mantel with a mirror. Scotch-tape a frame of tinsel around the mirror, the heaviest tinsel you can find or use a double row if need be. On the mirror itself rubber-cement a snowstorm of glittering sequins (later the rubber cement will rub off easily). Select a pair of branched candlesticks—those made of wire are admirable for the purpose. Wind them with tinsel. (A bit of Scotch tape at the end of each piece will secure it.) Hang tiny colored balls here and there on the candlesticks. Stand your candles in place. And place the candlesticks so that the candle flames will give sparkle and brilliance to the sequin snowstorm.

CHRISTMAS TABLES. Some of the suggestions given under Christmas mantels, and some of those which will come later under other headings, may be adapted for the Christmas dinner table. And vice versa. But here are a number of special suggestions for tables which you may like.

Floating Flowers: This is, I think, a charming and inexpensive table decoration, one which is easy to do, and

13. A charming and easy-to-achieve arrangement of heather and pink carnations graced by flower tapers which run from pale pink to deep mauve. Candles by Colonial Candle Company. Photograph courtesy of Franklin Advertising Service.

14. An always-green setting for a pillar candle – the intriguing Candle Planter Bowl in copper and brass. From The Candle Light, Fair Haven, New Jersey.

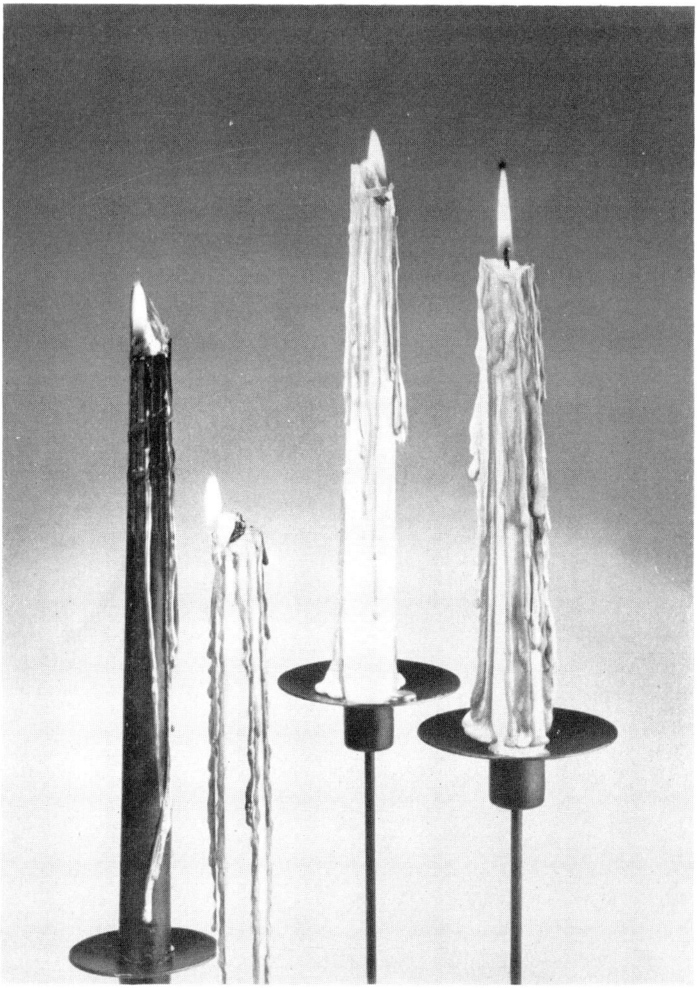

15. Black that drips gold; white that drips silver, scarlet, or seven different colors—these candles spill their colored wax in particularly pleasing fashion. Candle by Ho-Car.

16. A kitchen garden conversation piece—the candles to harmonize with the chopping-block-and-vegetable décor. A red rose for the final fillip. Setting by Margaret Carrick, California.

17. Tall creamy beeswax candles which hold light within themselves; a yellow-toned spring bouquet in a green-blue glass container. Setting by Margaret Carrick, California.

18. For Easter entertaining: pink and yellow tapers in black metal holders, a basket full of flowers, an iron wire chicken basket holding colored eggs. Setting by Margaret Carrick, California.

19. For the entrance hall at Christmas time: welcoming candles in tin Mexican candlesticks; a charcoal pottery bell spilling bright-hued balls. Setting by Margaret Carrick, California.

20. A fat pink candle in a black wire candle ball, a from-your-garden arrangement of dahlias in a matching vase. Setting by Margaret Carrick, California.

21. Creamy white and delicate pink candles in a setting of frosty evergreens. The collector's-item Christmas decorations suspended nearby you can make yourself. Setting by Margaret Carrick, California.

22. Three white Taperlite candles dominate a supper setting. The dark green cloth provides a striking contrast for candles, pastel flowers and bone china. Candles and setting by Will & Baumer.

23. A snack buffet is highlighted by gay yellow Twistolites in turquoise pottery holders. Chrysanthemums, grapes and gourds form the centerpiece. The cloth is pale yellow. Candles and setting by Will & Baumer.

24. White Twistolite candles in green Bristol lusters on the table—green Taperlites on the chest in the background. The centerpiece is arranged in a "cardinal's hat"—this one once used by Ethan Allen. Candles and setting by Will & Baumer.

25. Dinner for two, softly lit by white Twistolite candles in massive Moorish candlesticks. Asters and purple grapes are arranged in an antique stove top. Setting and candles by Will & Baumer.

can be fitted to almost any table. You will want a low round bowl—or a rectangular one, for that matter, if it suits your table better. Even a cake pan will do, but it should not be so small that it is lost in the center of the table. Stud the outside thickly with small Christmas-tree balls, rubber-cemented in place. Set the bowl in the center of the table, and circle it with tinsel, winding it around to form a tinsel mat, and tucking the end of the tinsel out of sight. Fill the bowl with water, and in it float several poinsettia candles, and a few silver Christmas-tree balls.

Then, if you like, make ready a set of individual bowls—about the size of finger bowls—one for each guest. Cover the bowls with rubber cement, and then with bead-sized Christmas-tree balls (they come in strings). Float a poinsettia candle in each, and when the main course has been cleared, and before the dessert is served, bring in these individual candles, lighted, and place them on silver-paper doilies at each place. Then your dessert and coffee—by candlelight.

Blue Snow: You will want one large blue snowball candle, and five small ones. (If your shop does not have them in blue, recoat them with blue wax snow, as explained in Chapter 1.) Cover the sides of a round chopping block with tinsel, the top with a silver-paper doily. Set this in the center of your table. Place the large snowball on the decorated chopping block. Place the smaller snowballs, each on a small silver-paper doily, at intervals around the block, and a few inches away from it (the distance will depend on the size of your table). From the base of each small candle, to near the top of the large candle, run a strand of tinsel slightly curved. Pin it in place with glitter-tipped corsage pins. The effect is very gay, and the soft light from the snowball candles, most attractive.

Christmas-Tree Table: Place a large Christmas-tree candle on a gold lace-paper doily in the center of the table. Around this arrange a circle of small Christmas-tree candles—about eleven of them, each on a small gold doily, these overlapping to form a solid circle. From the bases of the small tree candles to the lower branches of the large one, run very fine tinsel, or gold cord to which you have glued sequins.

Holly and Spice: Coat the outside of a low, round bowl with rubber cement, and cover with gold glitter. (It rubs off easily, but during the rubbing-off process protect your hands with gloves, for glitter is, after all, ground glass.) In the bowl, arrange spicy white carnations and glossy-leaved holly with rich red berries. (Add artificial berries if need be.) Decorate about five gold lace-paper doilies by gluing small red Christmas-tree balls in a circle around the edges. Place the doilies around the bowl. In the center of each stand a pure-white vigil light.

Mirror Magic: You will need a round mirror, about 15 inches in diameter, and a wire-mesh flower holder. Cover the holder closely with Christmas-tree balls—the smaller sizes, but not all the same size. Wire them on, as many as possible. Select eight or nine flower tapers, in shades to harmonize with the balls. Cut the candles to approximately 12-inch lengths, and insert them, porcupine-fashion, in the bedecked flower holder. Glue a ring of Christmas-tree balls around the mirror. And set the candles in the center.

Angels and Stars: You will need five angel candles—dime stores and candle shops have them; five star-shaped candleholders; one large snowball candle and a glass bowl which, inverted, will make a well-proportioned base for the snowball candle. Stud the outside of the snowball candle with gold and silver sequin stars, pinned on. Invert the bowl and the candleholders and glue to the outside a sprinkling of the stars. Place the inverted bowl in the center of the table on a gold lace-paper doily. Stand the snowball candle on it, securing it with melted wax. Fasten the angel candles to the inverted stars in the same way (you don't want to take any chance on their slipping), and stand them in a ring around your centerpiece. The snowball candle burns throughout dinner. The angel candles may be lighted when dessert is served.

Sunburst Decoration: You will want a pale-pink pillar candle about 10 inches tall; an individual piepan, enough branches of long-needled pine to fan out in a circle around the base of the candle. You will need about two-dozen pieces of metallic ribbon, 9 to 15 inches long (depending on the size of your table), and in a variety of colors—gold, silver, pale-green, pink, ice-blue, lavender. You will also want coin dots, sequin stars, and small Christmas-tree balls in colors to go well with the ribbons.

Begin by gluing a ring of Christmas-tree balls around the piepan which is, quite simply, going to serve as the candleholder. With a table knife, mark out a small circle in the center of your cloth (this is merely to act as a guide). Pin the ribbons, sunburst-fashion, out from this circle, alternating colors and lengths. At the outer tip of each ribbon, fasten a small Christmas-tree ball. Place the decorated piepan at the center of the sunburst, and fan the pine needles out from this—over the ribbons. (The ribbons should be longer than the feathery needles.) Stand the pink pillar candle in place, and heap some extra Christmas-tree balls around it in the piepan. Now sprinkle the coin dots and stars on the pine, letting a few of them drift to the cloth. And it takes longer to tell about this effective setting than to do it!

Angel-Cake Caper: Not the cake, of course, but the cake pans, the individual ones. Four of them. And four flat paper or metal candleholders, made from a circle of paper or metal with a holder in the center. Pans will fit over them. Decorate the outside of the pans with a snowflake sprinkling of sequins. Fill the pans with small Christmas-tree balls. Set the pans over the holders. Stand the candles in place. And march the finished decorations down the center of the table with a lacy arrangement of short, flat cedar branches between them. Simple as that.

Christmas Wreath: For a base, cut a ring from cardboard 13 to 15 inches in diameter, depending on the size of your table. At intervals around it, glue five flat metal or cardboard candleholders. Then cover the wreath with pine, festoon it with strings of Christmas-tree balls, tuck in a few clusters of red berries. Add a wide red-satin bow—in short, make a Christmas wreath. Place this in the center of the table, and stand red candles in the holders.

Poinsettia and Rose: Arrange cut red poinsettias and white roses in an oblong bowl, and place it in the center of the table. At each end stand three white vigil lights decorated with bands of gold braid at the base of each glass container. It's an elegant and lovely setting.

CHRISTMAS THROUGH THE HOUSE. Candles belong all over the house at Christmas. If you have a chandelier, festoon it with tinsel, hang it with Christmas-tree balls, give it a gala look. If you have wall sconces, set them with your finest tapers, decorate them with festoons of greens and Christmas-tree decorations. The sideboard will hold Christmas candles and the table in the entrance hall should have lighted candles to give a holiday welcome to all who enter.

Fluted Silver: Margaret Carrick does some lovely arrangements which are effective in halls or on sideboards. One, for instance, uses a shallow bowl mounted on a copper-wire tripod. In the center, she stands a tall, golden taper. Around this and over the bowl, she sets a circle of fluted silver paper. And on this at the candle base, she arranges a few sprigs of waxy mistletoe and an assortment of Christmas-tree balls: three large ones—pink, gold, and blue; smaller ones in gold and silver.

Styled with Candles: Another of her arrangements—and this is a particular favorite of mine—is shown in Color Plate III. Here a ball of white Styrofoam has been set on the lip of a tall Italian glass bottle. The candle, set into the top of the Styrofoam ball is raised to an impressive height. Feathery sprigs of buckwheat, touched with artificial snow, are inserted in the Styrofoam to make a cloudlike drift around the candle. Mexican straw beads spiral down around the bottle carrying the color to the round red mat on which the whole arrangement is set. A snowball candle repeats the white ball at the top in a larger size and rougher texture. The snowball candle is placed on a square black base for accent in a shape different from all the circular forms.

Pageantry: Or take another favorite of mine (I seem to have a good many when it comes to discussing Mrs. Carrick's arrangements). This is a lovely one of creamy-white and delicate pink candles, set in copper Magic Circle holders, with white frosted evergreens around the base. The five candles are of various heights, the two tallest in creamy-white, the pinks ranging from pale to deep. And nearby hang three most handsomely decorated balls—the highest (and smallest) in deep-pink, the second in gold, the third (which is largest and lowest), a very pale-pink. These particular balls I should call collector's items—and inspiration for all who like to do their own decorating. They are splendidly jeweled, embellished with velvet and gold cord. (See Illustration 21.)

Postscript to decorators: You know, I am sure, that you can embellish ordinary Christmas-tree balls—thus making them even gayer—by gluing on sequins, metallic cord or braid, rhinestones and glitter. But for the collector's items which you may create why not work in Styrofoam, cork, or some similar product which will give you greater leeway —and permanency. Decorations may be pinned in place. Fine quill-like studding, for instance, can be done by threading a tiny bead on a pin, then a bugle bead—the pins then driven into the ball. Incidentally, such handsomely done decorations as this are, in themselves, lovely gifts.

Mexican Bell: Another of Mrs. Carrick's settings uses fat candles made by Mexican candlemakers in Los Angeles. The candles are set in finely crafted tin candlesticks. These are in two sizes and are fitted to teakwood stands. Nearby a giant charcoal pottery bell from Oaxaca is used in the manner of a cornucopia, spilling out an abundance of bright-hued Christmas balls in varying sizes and textures —some satiny smooth, some frosted. Sprays of blue spruce and a honey-colored mat complete the picture. Such an arrangement as this, I think, would make a warm welcome for the entrance hall. (See Illustration 19.)

Salad-Bowl Idea: On the hall table, stand a giant candle in the center of a large wooden salad bowl; then heap the bowl with colored balls. Flank the arrangement with evergreens, and nestle a few more balls among the boughs.

Sunburst Table: Patio candles do well in entrance halls. The glass containers protect them from gusts of wind when the front door is opened, and the flames don't flicker out. In Chapter 3 you will find any number of suggestions for decorating the patio candles. Select your favorite, and stand three at intervals along the hall table. From the base of each run a sunburst of gold and silver tinsel, Scotch-taped at the base of the candles at one end, under the edge of the table, or to the top, at the other end. Some of the sunburst lines will cross, making an allover pattern on the table top.

Or with the patio candles, use evergreens, holly and mistletoe at the base. Or place the candles on great snowflakes cut from paper foil. Or drift spun glass around the bases.

Magic Circles: For another entrance hall decoration, you might fashion a wreath of greens, deck it with ornaments, and hang it over the table. Toward one end of the table, and so that the arrangement will flank the wreath, stand seven candles of various colors and heights. Magic Circle holders do well here, for they will hold candles of different sizes, and can be grouped in combinations, as shown in Illustration 35.

Christmas-Gift Candle: For the hall table, choose a large, rough-textured, white candle, and decorate it with tiny Christmas-tree balls and festoons of sequins, pinned in place. Wrap and tie a gay assortment of miniature packages, and pile them around the candle base.

Table Sparkle: Use white-painted, gold-glitter-frosted bare twigs, sprigs of holly, a few stalks of gilded grain or grass for the floral arrangement. Flank this with red patio candles decorated with gold snowflakes, cut from paper doilies, and tiny red tree balls.

SIDEBOARDS AND BUFFETS. Moving out of the hall now, we might look first at a Will & Baumer setting, which you can easily copy. A sleek red Taperlite candle is placed in a wonderful tin Colonial candlestick. The floral decoration at its side is fashioned from evergreens, bright red gladiolus, cotoneaster berries, and a few pine cones. This is placed in front of a pewter plate, which will catch and hold the candle's soft light. (See Illustration 28.)

Pilsener Glass Trifles: Make unique buffet candleholders from Pilsener glasses. Dot them with gold stars (glued on), and don't forget to put some of the stars on the base of each glass. Rim a glass bobêche with tiny dangling Christmas-tree balls. (Run a gold cord through the wire hooks on the balls and glue the cord to the bobêche. Glue a small star over the ends of the cord for a neat finish.) Set the candles in the glasses, fastening them with melted wax. Put the bobêche in place. A row of these is gay and pretty.

Star, Bell, and Candle: Buy five star-shaped gelatin molds. Brush the outside of each with rubber cement, and cover with silver glitter. Fill with Christmas-tree balls, *gluing them in place.* Fasten a tiny gold bell to the points of each star. Suspend these by lengths of tinsel over the sideboard. (Just punch a hole in one star point and run the tinsel through it.) The first, third, and fifth star should be hung slightly higher than the second and fourth. All should be of a length to make a background for your candles. Cut three 8-inch silver stars from metallic paper. Place these on the sideboard, and stand an Emkay Star Pillar Candle in Christmas red in the center of each. The candles will burn throughout the holiday season, and the star decorations can be saved for use another year.

Gilded Fruit Tray: Spray fruit with gilt paint and let dry. A pineapple makes a wonderful central piece—and it can also be studded with tiny Christmas-tree balls. Apples, pears, lemons, and oranges may also be used, and to the last, glue a few sequins after the gilding. Add some shining green leaves. Arrange a trayful of the gilded fruit, and circle it with vigil lights set on small, gold, lace-paper doilies.

Finial Star: A pair of hurricane candles can be given a Christmas look in no time at all. Around the base of each, place gold or silver Christmas-tree finials—points out—to form a six-pointed star. In between, place a gay Christmas-tree ball.

Tinsel Spikes: Or set pillar candles on silver-paper doilies. Cut a ring of Styrofoam which will fit around the base of each. Gild the Styrofoam, and set it in place. Stick tinsel spikes into this, fanning up and out around the candles.

Now just to round out this Christmas picture, here are some final suggestions: Over a corner table festoon the wall with strings of pine cones and gold balls. On the table below set a brass candelabrum with red candles. . . . Or do an arrangement of driftwood, powdered with white snow. Add a few small red flowers. Set a red vigil light to illuminate the setting. . . . Or set carnation nosegays and small silver balls at the base of tall white tapers. Use an Arrange-O-Disc for your flowers. . . . And so ends our decorations for Christmas, when every candle burns with special meaning, and with special warmth and brightness.

Did you know that at the court of Louis XIV—and that was back in 1643 to 1715—a candle was never relighted? Once burned and snuffed out, the candle ends were given to the ladies-in-waiting, who quite often made more from selling them than they were paid as members of the court. Besides being a source of income for the ladies, candles were also a mark of favor for the gentlemen. There was a nightly ceremony when the King disrobed. A tall wax candle was held aloft while he knelt in prayer. Then King Louis solemnly chose the man he wished to honor, and the recipient proudly bore the candle away—and just as promptly sold it!

VALENTINE'S DAY. And a good time to mention some romantic notions not for exclusive use on February 14. Dining for two, for instance, and you might let red felt be your table cover. Use white pottery. Set your flower-and-candle arrangement off center (better for tête-à-tête dining). The flowers might well be pink carnations in a low bowl. Behind them a semicircle of white tapers in low white ceramic holders.

Bridge Party: Make cloths of pastel organdy for the tables. Ruffles around the edge, and put a plain white cloth on the table first. In the center, stand a spring-green or dusty-pink Emkay Twisted-Pillar Candle, set on a small round tray or plate. On tray or plate, and around the candle, put a ring of Non-spillable Water cut to fit. Set in this whatever delicate flowers your florist has. Use a bit of ivy with them and let it twine a little way up the candle.

Heart Valentines: Cut a Styrofoam heart and deck it with sequins, gold and silver lace, cupids—in short, turn it into a fabulous valentine. Cut slim red flower tapers to

8- or 10-inch lengths, and set them around the rim of the heart, angling them out a little.

Or cut a heart from a block of Non-spillable Water. Mold the tip in silver foil. Wire to the base of a tapering pillar candle—in red or white. Stud the heart—on both sides—with red and white carnations (very short stems) to make a valentine design.

EASTER. And we begin, of course, with simple and elegant arrangements of white candles and spring flowers. You will find a number of flower-and-candle ideas earlier in the chapter which can well be adapted.

Breakfast Party: If you wish a gayer note, you might copy Margaret Carrick's Easter specialty. A black wire basket in the form of a chicken holds a gay array of colored eggs. Nearby a natural straw basket tipped on its side holds pink, yellow, and lavender flowers. (The basket may conceal a container, or you could use Non-spillable Water.) The tapers, set in black metal holders with shining spiral tops, are in pink and yellow. (See Illustration 18.)

Easter Eggs: If you have one of those wonderfully decorated sets of nested eggs, you can use them for a special Easter arrangement. Set candles in the bottom halves of the eggs (a bit of wax to secure them), and the candles will range from large to small, just as the eggs do. Place them in a row, and in front of them stand the upper halves of the eggs.

Easter Bunny: Or cut a bunny from Styrofoam. Give him sequin eyes and pipe-cleaner-decked-with-glitter for whiskers. Rouge his ears faintly pink. And give him a pink taper to hold between his paws.

Bird Cage: Or do an arrangement of flower tapers and spring flowers set in a gilded bird cage for an Easter-season party centerpiece—or, for that matter, for any other spring occasion.

SUMMER. Don't eliminate summer-time use of candles, but do keep your arrangements "cool." There is nothing drearier than wilting candles on a hot day—and candles are far too lovely to treat so cruelly. Try some of these summertime ideas:

Summer Sea: In the center of the table, set a low, round, clear glass bowl. Fill it with water colored a beautiful blue-green with vegetable coloring. Float three white flower candles in the water's cool-looking depth.

Flame and Ice: Or set a flower and candleholder in the bottom of a clear glass bowl—a good-sized round one. In it set ice-blue flower tapers. Heap the bowl with artificial ice cubes—they're sold at novelty shops. Set the arrangement on a frosted mirror.

Fern Fronds: Or ring a round mirror with fern fronds, tucking them under the edge of the glass. In the center of the mirror set a small, fluted bowl of clear glass. Float a delicately tinted flower candle in this bowl. On the mirror, place four more flower candles, but light only the one in the bowl.

Frosted Fancy: Or do a cool, kitchen-garden arrangement in a silver-metal bowl, set on a frosted mirror. Use shiny green peas in the pod, green peppers, a few green beans. Trail a little of the garden bouquet over the mirror. Add a few strands of trailing ivy to soften the pattern of the arrangement. At each side, set a vigil light, the glass finger-painted in a fernlike pattern in green.

Dining at Dusk: If you are dining late and dusk has come, do eat by candlelight—at least on occasion—but set the candles on the sideboard. Use cool colors for the candles, and delicate arrangements for the flowers. Seascapes (already mentioned in this chapter), give an illusion of coolness. And for dining out of doors—porch, backyard, or patio—do use patio candles. The wind won't blow them out, and for dining-at-dusk which most of us prefer on summer evenings, the soft, flickering light seems exactly right.

HARVEST-TIME ARRANGEMENTS. With warm rich colors, fruit and grain, bright autumn flowers. Some of the flower-and-candle settings mentioned in this chapter do well here. You might use grapes and gourds and a few bright fall leaves for the centerpiece, and tapers in deep-green and wine to flank it. Or fill a lettuce basket with shining red tomatoes, green peppers, and trailing strands of ivy. Flower tapers for the candles.

Horn of Plenty: You could copy a Norma Simpson setting, using Emkay Horn of Plenty candles and green grapes against a dark-green cloth. She has flanked two of the larger candles with the grape clusters and a few green leaves, and then uses small matching candles at individual place settings. (See Illustration 33.)

Pineapple Pretty: Lady Brett gives us a simple-as-can-be setting done with a pineapple—decorative fruit that it is—grapes, and citrus fruits, clustered around two similarly decorated Lady Brett candles. To complete the picture: a graceful decanter, a leaf-patterned plate. (See Illustration 29.)

Color Spill-over: Ho-Car, makers of unique self-decorating candles which through a patented process spill the multicolored wax over the candles in a particularly pleasing fashion, sets a charming autumn buffet with a deep-green cloth and low brass candelabra. Let these flank a floral setting of gold-and-bronze chrysanthemums, handsomely arranged. (See Illustration 15 for Ho-Car candles.)

Moorish Night: Or if you are in a dinner-for-two mood, you might choose two white Will & Baumer Twistolite candles, and set them in massive Moorish brass candlesticks. Asters and purple grapes are arranged in an antique stove top on the polished table, with the place settings on charcoal linen mats. (See Illustration 25.)

Halloween: Set the party buffet, as Norma Simpson does, with Emkay ghosts and black cats cavorting around a piece of driftwood. Or you might turn a pumpkin into both centerpiece and candleholder by boring holes in it, and "spiking" it with slim flower tapers. Set the pumpkin on a round inverted tray or a bed of glossy green leaves. . . . And a ring of shiny red apples set on a round mirror can become your candleholders. Bore holes in them as you would for baking, and fit the holes with a cup of foil. Use candles which are not more than 6 inches tall—in yellows, greens, russet, orange-red.

Thanksgiving: You may want to borrow from some of the settings already suggested, or you might do an attractive centerpiece with a tall rope pillar candle set in a low bowl on a round tray. Arrange pompons in the bowl around the base of the candle, wiring them to the candle so that they form a mound. Then around the bowl, on the tray, make a ring 3 or 4 inches wide of various kinds of unshelled nuts. Gild a few of them. Add some cranberries and sprigs of green leaves for the finishing touch.

Rural Scene: You might do a rural scene on a rectangular tray in the center of the table: rustic fence—cut from cardboard, fashioned from skewers, or borrowed from your child's toy box; sponge bushes, miniature shocks of corn. And within the scene set Emkay's Big Tom Turkey candles.

Medley: Or arrange a centerpiece of gourds, polished apples, grapes, and unshelled nuts. Flank it with 9-inch candles in wine, green, and brown. . . . On the sideboard you might do an arrangement of dried grains and grasses with sprigs of orange-red berries. At each side set Emkay's Harvest Corn candles. . . . Or set a row of Will & Baumer's white Twistolite candles along the back of the sideboard. In front of them, do a long oval arrangement using feathery white chrysanthemums, yellow pompons, and red seed pods of sumac. . . . Or let the sideboard arrangement be of goldenrod, ageratum, dried grasses, and gray-green milkweed pods. At each side, place a curved, three-branched candelabrum holding one pale-yellow candle, one of deep-yellow, and one of soft-brown.

And since we've been around the calendar, through all kinds of weather, did you know that candles can foretell the weather? When their flames snap, or burn with a dim or unsteady light, rain and frequently wind will follow. It may not be an absolute rule, of course—but is any weather rule absolute?

26. An early American setting for a bayberry candle with its sweet scent and soft light. The foliage: cotoneaster. Candle and setting by Will & Baumer.

27. A formal arrangement for the mantel, featuring fall flowers and golden yellow Twistolite candles. Candles and setting by Will & Baumer.

28. A tin Colonial candlestick holds a sleek red Taperlite candle: evergreens, bright red gladioli and cotoneaster berries are backed by a pewter plate.

29. A made-to-order match, with pineapple and citrus fruit decorating the candles. Both candles and setting by Lady Brett.

30. Summer-day suggestion: Delicately tinted candles with only the one floating in the cool crystal bowl lighted. Candles and setting by Lady Brett.

31. and 32. A selection of the unusual "special occasion" candles now available in shops—or for those who wish to have their own shops. These from The Candle Light, Fair Haven, New Jersey.

33. For autumn dining, Horn of Plenty candles and green grapes against a dark green cloth. Candles by Emkay. Setting by Norma Simpson.

34. The feature attraction is the Prism candle (center) which transforms itself into sculptured beauty as it burns. Setting by The Candle Light, Fair Haven, New Jersey. Prism candle by Victrylite Candle Company.

35. Decor-Lite's Magic Circle holders fit all candles. They may be used singly or in groups. Candle decorators find them useful for base-of-the-candle wreath decorations. Waxed flowers, miniature fruit and vegetable decorations, and so on, may be wired to them.

36. A corner of one of the country's best-known candle shops—began originally in the corner of a grocery store, now housed in six rooms and with an international trade. The Candle Light, Fair Haven, New Jersey.

How far that little candle throws his beams!
So shines a good deed in a naughty world.

SHAKESPEARE

V

Money-Making Matters

HOW TO START A CANDLE BUSINESS IN YOUR HOME OR SHOP

YOUR FLAIR for making and decorating candles can bring you profits as well as pleasure. A good many women throughout the country have already found candlecraft a means to extra income, and they lay no claims to special genius or a mysterious "talent for business." They have ability, yes—the same kind you have which leads friends to admire your work. That and a few simple rules dictated by common sense will get you started. And in your kitchen laboratory and dining-room studio, your leisure-time activities may bring you in a pretty penny.

Let's consider first making money from the candles which you decorate—commercial candles or homemade. Having decided that you would like to let this craft earn you some money you are, so to speak, in business. You have already served your apprenticeship—by making candles for yourself and for your friends. You've practiced your hobby to perfect it. You know that you can do the job. Enough practice so that you are sure—before you write a price tag or take an order.

You need no special shop to launch you in business. No larger workroom than you already have—whether that be dining room table, corner of the sunporch, or part of the basement playroom. You will not suddenly lay in imposing supplies of wax, crayons, commercial candles, and decorations. At first your orders will change very little from what they have been. Most thriving home businesses have had humble beginnings. Some, of course, grew so large that they literally pushed their originators out of kitchen or parlor and into *big* business. Hazel Bishop was a student at Columbia University when she worked out the formula for her nonsmear lipstick. At first she sold only a few hundred dollars' worth. Now her sales measure in the millions. Arthur P. Chamberlain was a Wall Street broker whose hobby was puttering around his home workshop. His knack for mending things turned him into the Mending Man of Greenwich, Connecticut, with a highly profitable annual business. Thousands tell the same story.

Some like Alice Jaffe, mentioned before in this book, purposely keep their home businesses small. Mrs. Jaffe has had many opportunities to increase sales of her beautifully decorated candles and "go commercial." Frequently she has had to turn down orders because she wants to keep hers a home business, and only for her spare time. Many women—probably most of you who read this book—will want to follow her system. Others may eventually wish to let their businesses expand. But in either case, the start is the same.

When the first friend has admired a candle you have

made, or the first dinner guest has remarked on the charm of candles you have decorated, you have taken the first step toward making your craft a success. You have created something someone else *likes.*

The second step, even more important, is that your creation has become something someone else *wants.* When you give a friend a pair of candles you have decorated, and later she begs to buy a pair, when someone asks you to decorate candles for a wedding reception or church supper, you are setting a firm foundation for your home business. This kind of advertising is not as splashy as a big ad in the *Times,* not as attention-getting as a spot on radio or TV—but it's far more practical for your purpose.

One mistake the beginning home-businesswoman often makes is to try for volume orders too soon. If they come in, the little kitchen workshop is swamped, orders stack up, deliveries are late. Perhaps extra help is hired to stem the tide—and the profits vanish. Far better to begin as Mrs. Julia Stevens Kraft did with the fudge made on her wood-burning range in her farmhouse kitchen. She carried it, a few bags at a time, to the local baker to sell for her. The ten-cent-per-bag profit she made gradually grew to a fabulous business. *Gradually* is the word to underline.

TIME YOURSELF. Before you send out any formal announcements, there are a number of things you should do:

For one, keep records of how long it takes you to make various types of candles: flower-trimmed, glitter-decorated, etc. Select half a dozen basic types for the test (and this is true either for making candles or decorating commercial candles). Keep an accurate record of your time for each.

With a little experience, you will be able to estimate times for either simpler or more complicated candles. But don't guess. The it-takes-about-ten-minutes, or I-can-do-that-in-about-an-hour kind of planning, will lead you into trouble on two counts: You will underestimate your time and take more orders for a given delivery date than you can manage (and believe it or not, people almost always underestimate the amount of time it takes them to accomplish any interesting task—including decorating candles). And in your pricing, you will not allow a proper return for your time.

Pin-money business or big business—either must not only give you a margin of profit over costs, but must repay you for your time. Many people beginning a home business have a tendency to "throw in their time." Somehow or other they seem to grow embarrassed over the idea of charging for the time they use to "do something they really enjoy, anyway." The same woman, no matter how much she enjoyed doing teaching or secretarial work would not dream of "throwing in her time." Home candlecraft is no different. Basically you have two things to give to your business: ability and time. Both are valuable.

Figure out how much time a week you wish to—and can—give to your business. You have a home to run, obligations to meet, recreational and social activities which are important to you. You don't want your part-time business to encroach on your family life. And perhaps that is rule number 1 for the part-time home business. The family will take part—a lot in pride and a little in help—but they will not want to give you up to wax and wicks, to sequins and glitter. So plan your work time with all this in mind, and—except on those rare occasions which prove the rule—keep your work within stated work hours.

You now know how much time it takes to make and/or decorate representative candles, and you know how many hours a week you wish to give. From these two facts you can figure out just about how many orders you can handle comfortably. Generally speaking, don't go beyond this. There will, of course, be those times when good customers all seem to want special candles the same week—and all with reasons which brook no delay. During those weeks, time schedules go out the window. You put in overtime.

SELLING PRICE. Pricing your candles should not be a hit-or-miss proposition. When you figure your selling price, you must take into account *all* costs for supplies: wax, wicks, molds, and crayons if you are making candles; the cost of commercial candles if you are buying them to decorate. *All* supplies used in decorating must be included —and just because there are "only a few sequins," or "just one paper doily," don't skip them. One pair of candles using these items may not make much difference. But if you keep on leaving out such expenses "because they are so little," over the course of a year they may well be the items which make your part-time business all work and no pay. Add to your total costs a *fair* wage for yourself. Then add the desired markup. This will give you your selling price.

There is no way to set an exact percentage markup for you. You will be governed partly by prices which those in your particular locality are willing to and can pay. In some places, this will be higher than in others. And for some candles your markup can be greater than for others.

For instance, the markup will be less on a simple, attractive candle than it will be on a unique and highly original one. And this is not because the former costs you less or can be done in a shorter time. As a matter of fact, the latter candle could take no more time, and use even less expensive materials. But, since it is more creative, it is more valuable as an artistic achievement. The ideas which you have put into it are worth more. Your customer will recognize this and pay accordingly. You, too, will recognize this and charge accordingly.

Don't be embarrassed over charging for your skill any more than for your time—even though your first customers may be friends. Frequently beginners in a business feel they should not include skill when setting a price. Probably they would be among the first to argue against a similar practice on the part of others. We all sell our skills—whether they are the nimble fingers of a good file clerk, the pleasant voice of a telephone operator, the executive abilities of a businessman. Or the creative talent which goes into decorating a beautiful candle. Naturally you won't want to set the markup so high that no one can afford to buy your candles—much as they would like to. But neither will you want to make it so small your profit is barely visible.

HOW TO BUY. Part of the success of a home business—as in any other—depends on wise buying. Since you are going to start in a modest way, you will not be able to take advantage of price cuts offered for volume buying. You will have to base your costs on retail prices, for those are what you will be paying. Later, if your business expands, you can buy in quantity. Meanwhile, your local merchants may offer you discounts, and you should contact manufacturers to see whether or not the amounts you buy warrant a wholesale price.

In the meantime, practice the same buying techniques as in your household marketing. When there is a sale of articles you use, stock up. Take advantage of the best prices. If one store sells at slightly less than another, buy there—and do take time to canvass stores in your area so you will know where the best values are.

In a profitable business operation, there must be enough margin between cost and selling price to cover operating expenses and *net profit*. The spread between the cost of goods and the selling price is called the *gross margin*. The usual merchandising equation is figured this way: Sales price is set at 100 per cent. From this, subtract the cost of goods (which includes transportation charges if they are to be paid). The figure left after subtracting is called the *gross margin*. Subtract from this figure *all* operating costs—including your own wages. Whatever is left is your *net profit*. For example:

	Per cent	*Dollars*
Sales price	100	$10.00
Cost of goods	—55	5.50
Gross margin	45	4.50
Operating expenses	—30	3.00
Net profit	15	1.50

This is a little formula to remember should you ever start expanding your home business. Don't guess about whether or not you are making a profit. It's a human failing when there is a twenty-dollar bill in the till to look at it in admiration, forgetting that over the past six weeks you have spent x dollars and x hours to earn that twenty dollars. Figure out your net profit regularly. Then you will know in hard-to-evade figures just what profit you are making—and whether or not your business is worth while.

DO KEEP RECORDS. Even if yours is the smallest possible home business, keep records. Without records you don't really have a business. Your records do not have to be complicated—quite the contrary. But they must be accurate. Keep track of every single penny you spend, and don't trust your memory, or count on a hazy recollection of "about five dollars." Let's take the Net Profit Formula just given. But this time, let's say that your records were poor, and that you *guessed* the cost of goods was $5.50 when the figure *should have been* $6.50. Let's say that you guessed operating expenses at $3.00 when in reality they were $5.00. Here's how it would work out:

	Dollars
Sales price	$10.00
Cost of goods	—6.50
Gross margin	3.50
Operating expenses	5.00
Net profit	—1.50

And a minus $1.50 for a net profit is an unhappy state of affairs! So be accurate in your records—both as to what you make and what you spend.

But don't get the feeling that bookkeeping and figuring are going to take all the pleasure out of your candlecraft business. The simplest kind of ledger will do. Dime and stationery stores have them. Jotting down your purchases —and your sales—in the account book becomes a habit and you automatically set down money spent on return from a shopping tour. Don't let sales slips pile up so that one day you find yourself faced with a stack of unentered bills and mysterious figures on scraps of paper. It's rather like dresser drawers or closet shelves. If you let them go week after week, tidying them becomes a chore. If you keep them neat as you go along, the problem solves itself. So will your record keeping.

ABOUT TAXES. There is a little matter of taxes. From the United States Department of Commerce, Finance and Tax Division, Washington, 25, D. C., you can get a booklet called: *Basic Tax Information for Small Business Enterprises.* Your pin-money business may not find itself affected—but if or when your business begins to grow, you will need this information. You should also write to your state capitol to inquire about state taxes, and check up on local taxes—sales tax, for instance, or license taxes. And while you are checking with your local government, ask about possible zoning laws which might affect you. The chances are that none will, but it's easier to find out than to guess and be wrong.

BUILDING YOUR BUSINESS. You began, quite probably by selling a few candles here and there to friends who admired your work. Maybe these first sales were more labors of love than business, and you charged only for materials. But when you decide to put your candlecraft to work for you, then—friends or no—set your prices as already indicated.

To launch your business, you might send out informal notes to friends and acquaintances. Say that you are now taking orders for candles, and that you hope—if they should ever want specially decorated ones—they'll be interested in yours. Include a price list for four or five different types of candles. Add a line saying that you will be glad to quote prices for special orders. Give your address and telephone number.

Initially this may be all that you wish to do. It will give you a testing period—to see whether or not you have estimated your time and prices correctly—and a chance to get your working habits in order. But at the same time start keeping notes which will help you expand your business. Keep records of anniversary and birthday dates. The local paper will help you on this with their reports of anniversary and birthday parties. When these special dates come around, write to those concerned a few weeks in advance, asking whether or not they might like special candles for the occasion.

Make any note or card you send look professional. Plan what you have to say so that your copy is clear and concise, interesting but not wordy. Arrange copy so that the layout is attractive—and consider it an advertising layout even though it is informal and hand-written. Having your name, address, and phone number printed on cards or note paper is a highly sensible idea, and can be done inexpensively.

CUSTOMER LISTS. Friends will help you build customer lists. Candles you sell them will be shown to their friends, and the word-of-mouth publicity will bring you new orders. When you hear of someone new who is interested, telephone that person, call on her, or send her a business note describing your services. You may wish to have advertising cards printed, or a circular done in photo-offset. Talk to your local printer. He will be glad to help and advise you.

If you hear that someone has admired a particular type of candle you might call with samples of similar candles. Telephone first for an appointment. It's no good arriving when a customer may be in the midst of preparing a dinner party, has a bad cold, or is planning to take the children to the dentist's. And it is probably unnecessary to say this, but do keep appointments promptly. Fifteen minutes late or ten minutes early is not quite good enough. Keep an appointment book. Be scrupulous about it. Such small things as this—if being on time *is* a small thing—will help or harm your business. And will also help to keep it running smoothly instead of into a muddle.

Someone once said: Never forget the nonessentials. It's a good rule—if not exact. There are, actually, no nonessentials, but we have a way of looking at the small details as though they were not worth fussing about. But they are, of course. Unless the minor details are tended to: trimmings ordered when needed and before you have run out, deliveries made on time, work space kept in order, working hours maintained—unless any and all such seemingly not-too-vital details are followed through carefully, a measure of chaos results. And you will be harassed. Peace of mind and smoothness of operation are inseparable twins. You need both to make your home business a success—and fun.

Keep a card index of customers. Note dates of orders, types of candles they like, any special interests they may have. It takes only a minute to fill out—and file!—a card. Check your index frequently. When you have new candles which you believe a customer might like, call her or send her a card. (Need I add that addresses and phone numbers belong on the cards, so you don't waste time looking them up?)

Cross-index your customer file with a date file. Under *dates,* make notations regarding purchases. Suppose, for instance, Mrs. Jones, who has bought gift candles from you, always gives a large party in June. Slip a card with her name, address, phone number, and the notation in the June file. And check the June file on the first of May. Call Mrs. Jones then. Perhaps she would like special candles for her party—and there you have a nice order.

Find out in advance—through friends and local papers—when showers, weddings, dinner parties, bridge parties, club and church affairs are to be held. Create candle ideas for such events—don't actually do the decorating, just be able to describe it, and perhaps show a candle you have on hand which is a good sample of your imaginative work. Then contact those who are giving the affair, and see whether or not they will give you an order. They may want to change your ideas somewhat, but that is a small matter.

Set certain times for receiving telephone calls—say 9 to 11 A.M., if these are hours when you can always be available. It's discouraging for a potential customer to have to try repeatedly to get you. And it is too bad for you to lose sales because the phone rang in an empty house. If or when your business expands, you may want to subscribe to a telephone service which will take messages at all hours of the day and night.

HOME DISPLAY. Your home will become a showcase for the candles you create. You can display them—on your mantel, on tables, the sideboard, in the hall. You may want to put up shelves in sunroom or sewing room. Do them in natural color or black so that the candles will show to advantage. And shelves or no, keep a few pairs of various types of candles on hand for last-minute customers. A drawer or two in a chest can be divided with heavy cardboard or strips of wood to make useful storage space.

Lining the spaces with foil is a good idea. If the summer is hot, keep extra candles in the basement!

SHOP DISPLAY. Florist, gift, hardware, or other local shops may be interested in displaying samples of your candles with a printed card telling where they may be ordered. Local merchants might also be interested in buying candles to sell in their shops, and this is going to put you into a different position—if you accept. The advantage is that you are spared all the business of customer lists and contacts, advertising, etc. Your price to the merchant will, of course, be lower than to your own customer, for he is assuming part of your overhead—and he, too, must make a profit. If you are interested in this type of selling, make a list of possible outlets, and talk the idea over with the owners or buyers in question. Word of warning: Don't agree to supply more candles than you can safely manage.

CHRISTMAS SELLING. This will be one of your biggest seasons—so start early making Christmas candles, and getting orders. Not later than September and earlier if your customer list is large. Foil- or tissue-wrap finished products. Attach a card to each package describing the candle, and store by kind: holly-trimmed, sequin-trimmed, patio candles, etc.

If your own customer lists have not supplied you with all the Christmas orders you can handle, you might run an ad in the local paper during the first week in November. Plan it carefully. Simplify copy. Include all essential details. Don't accept more orders than you can handle. You can cover yourself in the ad with "a limited number of orders are being taken."

IF YOU EXPAND. The day may come when you want to establish a shop—or to share one with somebody. At this point order from the Government Printing Office (Washington 25, D. C.) their booklet: *Establishing and Operating a Gift and Art Shop,* also their *Gift and Art Shop Work Sheets* for estimated capital requirements. (There is no available material on candles alone.) Inquire about the field offices of the U. S. Department of Commerce (Washington 25, D. C.). Write to your nearest field office for advice. The Department publishes such booklets as *Accounting, Basic Information Sources, Basic Tax Information for Small Business Enterprises, Record Keeping for Retail Stores,* and *The Small Businessman and His Financial Statements.* The cost is nominal—or nothing—depending on the booklet.

If you plan to expand, do talk to the local banker and also the head of your local Chamber of Commerce. Their advice will be valuable—and a good balance wheel.

It is very doubtful that you will ever want to try to establish a shop where your stock is limited only to candles you make and/or decorate. One person's output would hardly stock a shop—and in many localities there would not be enough demand for such special candles to support it. Candlecraft is, in my opinion, for the leisure-time, home business. If you want to start a shop, it might be a gift or book shop—with candles included. A florist might be interested in sharing his shop with you—flowers and candles do go well together!

Or perhaps you would like to have a candle shop—a candle shop where you could include your own creations—but would also carry a wonderful array of commercial candles.

UNUSUAL COMMERCIAL CANDLES. As a candle decorator, you are, by this time, well acquainted with the fine variety of what we might call standard candles commercial companies produce. Many of them have been mentioned in this book. Do you also know about the enormous number of unusual candles which are available?

There are valentine place card candles—lovebirds perched on a circle of birch log decorated with forget-me-nots; Irish figure candles in native dress; Dutch girls; French figurines; Scotch lads and lassies; cowboys and cowgirls. There are, for Easter, choirboys, tulip and hyacinth candles, yellow ducklings, and bashful rabbits (including Peter himself—who was not so bashful). There are Easter eggs, fawns as young as spring, bunny girls, and sculptured flowers.

You can buy hand-carved rosebud candles; and pure white Glolite candles with pink carnations hand-painted on them. There are baby candles ranging all the way from cradles and bootees to baby bottles. There are such small-fry items as Goldilocks and the bears, Red Riding Hood and the wolf, Jack and Jill, Mary and her lamb, and the three little pigs.

Floating candles are not limited to water lilies. You'll find daffodils, poppies, crocuses, poinsettias; to go with them: plump green frogs, a family of turtles, a pair of ducks.

You can buy candles shaped like footballs, bowling pins, and bowling balls. Candles that look like ears of ripe corn. There are bridge-set candles. Liquor bottles. A pineapple candle which will act as an hors d'oeuvre holder for a cocktail party. There are special candles for weddings, anniversaries, and showers—ranging from bridesmaids to wedding bells.

There are nautical candles, sea gulls, and lighthouses. Come Halloween, you can get pumpkins, cats, and ghosts. For Thanksgiving, you'll find everything from John and Priscilla Alden to turkey candles. For Christmas the list is nearly inexhaustible.

In short, if you open a shop, you can include wonderful traditional candles—and a fabulous array of specialties. Illustration 32 shows just a few of them. From the Candle Manufacturers Association (19 West Forty-fourth Street, New York City, 36), you can get the names of candle manufacturers, who in turn will be glad to tell you what they have available, and what advertising matter they can offer for your use.

In Fair Haven, New Jersey, a cheerful, dark-haired woman has proved that turning a hobby into a business can be both profitable and fascinating. Her name, as we have said before, is Margaret Lo Piccolo—Peg Lo Piccolo to all who know her.

During World War II, Mrs. Lo Piccolo agreed to give her husband a hand with his grocery shop when help was short. But she made a bargain with him: She would help—if he'd let her have a corner of the store to display candles from her private collection. He had no objections. But very soon grocery customers were begging Peg Lo Piccolo for candles like hers, and it wasn't long before her husband complained that the candle business was crowding him out of the grocery business.

So Peg Lo Piccolo rented a cabin across the street and launched The Candle Light shop. From the single room where she began, that shop has grown to six rooms filled with every imaginable size, shape, color, and kind of candle. Customers from all over the country order from her. The shop is one of the most famous in the United

States. Tourists come to see the owner's private collection —which is the world's largest collection of hand-dipped, hand-carved, hand-painted, and hand-sculptured candles.

Peg Lo Piccolo's interest in candles dates back to the year she was seven. That year her father took her on a trip to Europe, and during the tour she visited the famous old Gautsch Wax Works—established over 360 years ago in Munich, Bavaria. Mr. Gautsch himself took the little girl on a tour of the Museum, and when she left, he gave her a miniature Nativity figurine, beautifully hand-carved by the wonderful craftsmen in the shop. She still has that candle, and it is the most prized in her collection of 2300 candles.

Today Peg Lo Piccolo not only manages The Candle Light, she lectures, does television shows, writes. Her business has grown from a corner in a grocery to a thriving enterprise with a $20,000 inventory. She believes others can do as well. (See Illustration 36.)

This is her story—the story of a woman who turned a hobby into a business and made it successful. Every year other women start along the same challenging path—some of them young women, some middle-aged, some who have reached what was once called the age of retirement. Every year other women start turning talent and leisure time into profits. Some in home businesses, which give them extra money they want, some in full-time enterprises, which grow and grow. It's an American story, written with energy and ingenuity, bringing a lot of satisfaction, and a lot of fun.

Success to *you*. May every candle you make or decorate bring pleasure to you. May any venture you undertake be rewarding. It has been good meeting you here by candlelight. And before we say good-by, there is one last quotation I should like to leave with you. It is inscribed on a small gravestone outside a British town blitzed during World War II. And its words carry a message of faith and of hope, and of strength—those enduring qualities which the flame of the candle has always symbolized:

> ☙ *There is not enough darkness in all the world to put out the light of one small candle. . . .*

INDEX

molds milk cartons wrap with adhesive tape.
two if tall one if short.

tin cans
Stand in ice to set base
Well which forms - note - save some
wax to fill in.
Floating - made in small tins

Rainbow kettle of warm water - tube oil paint
drop different colors on top. Do not stir. After
color spreads. Dip candle in & twirl.